TRIUMPH SPITFIRE & GT6
Setting the Small Sports Car Standard

John Nikas

Photography by Marc Vorgers

Dedicated to Mike Cook, who helped build the Triumph brand in America and kept the marque's flame burning bright into a new century.

First published 2019

Amberley Publishing
The Hill, Stroud
Gloucestershire, GL5 4EP

www.amberley-books.com

Copyright © John Nikas, 2019
Photographs copyright © Marc Vorgers

The right of John Nikas to be identified as the
Author of this work has been asserted in accordance with the Copyright, Designs and Patents Act 1988.

ISBN 978 1 4456 7448 3 (print)
ISBN 978 1 4456 7449 0 (ebook)

All rights reserved. No part of this book may be reprinted or reproduced or utilised in any form or by any electronic, mechanical or other means, now known or hereafter invented, including photocopying and recording, or in any information storage or retrieval system, without the permission in writing from the Publishers.

British Library Cataloguing in Publication Data.
A catalogue record for this book is available from the British Library.

Typeset in 10pt on 13pt Celeste.
Origination by Amberley Publishing.
Printed in the UK.

Appointed GPSR EU Representative: Easy Access System Europe Oü, 16879218
Address: Mustamäe tee 50, 10621, Tallinn, Estonia
Contact Details: gpsr.requests@easproject.com, +358 40 500 3575

Contents

1	Triumph and Travail	4
2	Birth of the Bomb	13
3	Under Pressure	33
4	Six Shooter	54
5	In Competition	80
	Bibliography	95
	About the Author	96
	About the Photographer	96

Chapter 1
Triumph and Travail

Triumph successfully weathered the perilous economic climate of the Great Depression, a dark period of declining sales and rising costs that had claimed several victims in the British motoring industry, but the firm foundered on the brink of total disaster as the Second World War drew near. After entering receivership during the summer, Triumph's assets were purchased by Thos. W. Ward Ltd, a steel and manufacturing conglomerate based in Sheffield. The news was announced to the public on 1 September 1939, mere hours after German soldiers crossed over the Polish frontier. Although the Triumph name eventually survived the war and flourished afterwards, little connection existed between the prewar and postwar versions of the company, which had once possessed an enviable reputation as one of Britain's most admired automotive and motorcycle manufacturers.

Bobbins and Wheels

Triumph evolved from a small firm that an entrepreneurial German émigré named Siegfried Bettmann established to import sewing machines built in Germany and the United States. Born in Nuremberg to merchant parents in 1863, Bettmann had moved to London shortly after his twenty-first birthday and found work as a clerk and translator for a small publishing house. After only six months, however, he had become bored and resigned to establish an office in Coventry as a foreign sales agent for the White Sewing Machine Company, based in Cleveland, Ohio.

While looking for additional products to supplement his existing catalogue, Bettmann decided to sell bicycles, which had fast become the nation's most

Siegfried Bettman, seen in the ceremonial robe that he wore as the Mayor of Coventry from 1913 to 1914, when he was the first non-British subject to hold the office. Although his Germanic roots forced his retirement after the start of the First World War, his contributions to his adopted homeland cannot be disputed. In addition to his important contributions to both Standard and Triumph, he also created a charitable foundation that helped individuals start their own businesses. (British Sports Car Hall of Fame)

popular form of personal transportation. Within a few months, bicycles were outselling sewing machines and to increase profits Bettmann found a firm in Birmingham that would supply him with inventory for sale under his own brand. Looking for a word that could be understood in various languages and would appeal to an international audience, Bettmann chose 'Triumph,' which soon became one of the most highly regarded names in the marketplace.

Triumph's success made an impact on others in the industry. Impressed with the firm's rapid growth, the Dunlop Pneumatic Tire Company provided Bettman with some capital investment in 1887, providing him with the necessary resources to expand the business. Later that same year, Bettmann formed a partnership with Mauritz Johann Schulte, a fellow German émigré, whose strategic vision supplemented his business acumen. To increase profits, the pair started to build their own bicycles, selling the first examples in 1889.

Even with Dunlop's previous investment, Triumph remained short on capital, a condition which would plague the company in the decades to come. With increasing consumer demand for bicycles, however, other investors soon appeared, allowing the company to form a German subsidiary called Orial Triumph Werke Nürnberg AG to handle European production in 1896.

Not long afterwards, however, consumer interest in bicycles fell as the popularity of motorised cycles increased. Blessed with a strong sense of the market, Schulte had already predicted this development and suggested that Triumph develop a motorbike to sell alongside the existing bicycle line. Although internal support for Schulte's proposal was strong, it took some time to develop a viable product, which delayed the arrival of the first Triumph motorcycle until 1902.

In those early days, Triumph, like other small manufacturers, lacked the means and production facilities to produce its own powerplants, forcing the company to use a Belgian Minerva one-cylinder engine that produced a scant 2¼ hp. The company continued to use third-party powerplants over the next three years, but a proprietary design finally appeared in 1905. The firm's new engine allowed the bike to cruise comfortably at 30 mph, and the simple construction kept the purchase price at an affordable level. With sales increasing each year, the company moved into new quarters in 1907, setting new sales records with the introduction of each successive model.

As the British Expeditionary Force readied to sail across the Channel in 1914, the War Office placed an order for 100 Model H motorcycles for immediate delivery. Although sold in essentially civilian trim, their stout construction and brisk performance endeared them to the British and Allied servicemen that rode them. By the end of hostilities, more than 30,000 examples had been delivered for military use, cementing the company's reputation in the process. Known as 'Trusty Triumphs', they were arguably the most popular motorbikes in military use and retained that vaunted position in the postwar civilian marketplace. Within two years, Triumph had become the best-selling motorcycle brand in England, generating sufficient profits to allow the perpetually underfunded operation to pursue automotive production for the first time.

Trusty Triumphs served across every front during the First World War, earning a reputation as the best motorcycles available during the conflict. This image shows Corporal Oswald H. Davis (far right) astride the Model H that he used to carry pigeons and deliver messages on the Western Front. (Philip Holdway-Davis)

Late to the Party

Following the Armistice, those motorcycle manufacturers that had not already added automobiles were making plans to do so, but Triumph hesitated, largely due to Bettmann's refusal to divert resources away from the profitable Model H. As early as 1903, Schulte had started to experiment with a motorised tricycle, but obtaining his partner's support and the resources to develop a viable motorcar proved elusive. Over the next fifteen years he continually pushed to build an automobile, but Bettmann refused to budge.

In 1919, the debate between the pair finally reached the boiling point, even as the company's engineers were working hard on a saloon prototype that showed great promise. Frustrated at the interminable delays in getting an automobile to market, Schulte departed the scene, denying Triumph his vision at a time when it was sorely needed. Even after his departure, automotive development continued, although at a greatly reduced pace, but other opportunities arose to hasten the process. In 1921, Triumph had the chance to acquire the assets of the struggling Morris operation, but Bettman refused to submit a bid, choosing instead to acquire the manufacturing facilities that had once belonged to the Dawson Car Company.

With all this happening behind the scenes, customers had to wait until 1923 for the first automobile from Triumph to arrive, which was designated the 10/20. Additional models followed, each larger and more sophisticated, featuring innovations such as hydraulic brakes and four-wheel dampers. The automotive press received them enthusiastically, pleased with their refinement and pleasant styling. Most customers, however, could not afford or did not want such large cars, forcing Triumph to design something smaller to appeal to the common man.

Although MG would eventually dominate the marketplace for small, affordable sporting cars, Triumph beat it to the punch when the diminutive Super Seven appeared in 1927. Similar in size and scope to Austin's Seven, it was stoutly constructed and reasonably fast, propelling it to instant success on the rally and trials circuit. Among the ranks of the drivers that won with the little car was Donald Healey, who had finished an impressive seventh overall in the Monte Carlo Rally and won several Gold Medals in a number of Triumphs.

Donald Healey seated in a saloon variant of the 1930 Triumph Super Seven. With several Triumphs held in the inventory at Healey's sales agency in Perranporth, the Cornishman became an enthusiastic supporter of the marque, often borrowing examples from the factory for competition use. This is the same vehicle that competed in the 1930 Monte Carlo Rally. (Walter Belgrove Collection)

Buoyed by the Super Seven's competition success and the subsequent publicity, Triumph started to expand the range, offering ten distinct models from family saloons to small coupés by 1930. Although demand for the smaller cars continued throughout the first years of the Great Depression, interest in the larger models began to wane. Rather than stand pat, Triumph pushed its product line further upmarket, introducing the Super Eight, Super Nine and Scorpion in 1932.

With nicer appointments and better performance, the new models were more expensive and complex, forcing the company into more competitive waters filled by more experienced and better-funded competitors. In order to increase sales, Triumph started to export cars throughout the British Commonwealth, where features such as right-hand steering, narrow bodies and lower top speeds were not seen as disadvantages as they were in America and on the European continent. Among the most important of these foreign markets were Australia and New Zealand, which Triumph recognised when the Southern Cross was introduced in 1932 – a name chosen to honour the iconic constellation visible only from the Southern Hemisphere.

The Healey Years
Bettmann retired rather reluctantly in 1933, thereby missing out on the introduction of the Gloria range, which would soon gain fame as the 'Smartest Cars in the Land'. Produced in a number of different versions, including sports cars, saloons, coupés and tourers, Triumph had gambled the future on their success. As the Glorias neared production, Triumph lured Donald Healey away from Riley to supervise development of the various models and manage the competition programme. Given his background, Healey focused the bulk of his attention on the sporting side of the ledger, helping to create the Monte Carlo Tourer, and even driving an example to a class win and a third overall finish in the 1934 Monte Carlo Rally. The unexpected result garnered significant media attention, with one motoring publication noting that 'Triumph has leapt into the front rank of famous marques'.

Jack Ridley in the passenger seat of the Dolomite Straight 8 at Brooklands, where the vehicle was extensively tested prior to its debut at the 1935 Monte Carlo Rally. Note that the headlamp pods have been turned aside in the interest of aerodynamic efficiency. (Graham Robson Collection)

Encouraged by Healey's success, Triumph decided to field an entry in the 2-litre sports class, allowing the upstart manufacturer to challenge some of the most famous marques in the world. Lacking the technical wherewithal or manufacturing experience to build such a vehicle from a clean sheet of paper, Healey took the advice of motoring journalist and close friend Tommy Wisdom, who suggested that Triumph replicate an existing vehicle rather than design one from scratch. The most obvious candidate was Alfa Romeo's 8C 2300, which was one of the most potent and successful sports cars on the market.

Healey obtained an example of the Italian sports car in London and had his technicians reverse-engineer the individual components, shortening the development process considerably. Once the work on the tool room copy was well underway, Healey travelled to Milan to secure blessing for his project from Vittorio Jano, Alfa Romeo's legendary chief engineer. Surprisingly, Jano assented almost immediately, honoured that a British company would want to build a replica of an Italian design.

Notwithstanding the obvious visual and technical similarities between the two cars, Triumph's Dolomite Straight 8 exhibited some important differences from the 8C 2300, incorporating a smaller 1,991cc engine, an Armstrong-Siddeley pre-selector gearbox, Hartford friction dampers, stronger leaf springs and Lockheed hydraulic drum brakes. It also featured a more robust chassis, since it was built for rally competition rather than road racing, which was the Alfa's speciality. Despite the derivative nature of the finished product, Triumph's Dolomite received almost universal praise from the motoring press following its introduction at the 1934 London Motor Show, representing a prime opportunity for Britain to build upon Bentley's previous competition dominance.

As events transpired, the Dolomite had an inauspicious debut, colliding with a train at an unguarded railroad crossing during the 1935 Monte Carlo Rally. Driving through a dense fog on the Jutland peninsula, Donald Healey slowed abruptly upon hearing a whistling sound, fearing that the supercharger was about to seize up. Instead, the noise that had caused him concern was an oncoming train that destroyed the car and almost killed both driver and navigator. Helping to make up for the near calamity, however, Jack Ridley finished second overall and won class honours in his Gloria Special, proving that Triumph could compete with the best in the field. The Dolomite returned to Monte Carlo the following year and finished eighth overall, which was the best showing for a British team, but management decided to abandon the expensive project to focus on more profitable models.

During the previous year, Triumph had taken a huge gamble, purchasing a new dedicated automotive production facility, but the move came at an inopportune time as sales fell even further, reducing the amount of money in the coffers. Even with fewer distinct variants to build in 1936 – several Gloria models having been discontinued – profits remained thin, forcing the sale of the motorcycle business to raise operating capital. Without the motorcycle profits to subsidize the automotive business, sales fell to fewer than 1,000 units, which worsened the financial picture considerably.

The introduction of a new model range, called the Dolomite to honour the Alfa-based competition car, helped boost sales temporarily, but demand soon fell back to earth. With no other alternative than to seek outside assistance, Donald Healey was named a company director and charged with finding a suitable merger partner. Promising discussions with Riley failed after the company accepted a better offer from Lord Nuffield, and then, following several abortive efforts to raise cash from other sources, Triumph entered receivership during the summer of 1939.

At the time that Triumph's assets were sold to Thos. W. Ward that fall, the new owners had planned to profit from the piecemeal sale of the company's individual assets, but the onset of war delayed those plans. Healey remained onboard as General Manager, supervising the transition into producing munitions for the war effort. Under his watch, the few workers that remained on staff focused on aircraft carburettor work and the excess space on the floor was rented out to manufacture fuselages for the Armstrong-Whitworth Albemarle.

From the Ashes
With so much of England's industrial capacity concentrated in Coventry and elsewhere in the West Midlands, the region became a priority for the Luftwaffe. There were several smaller attacks made during the Battle of Britain, but a massive bombing raid that took place during the night of 14 November 1940 caused unprecedented destruction. More than 500 bombers struck in the darkness, damaging most of the factories in the city and destroying more than 4,300 homes.

Triumph's original motorcycle factory, which had been under separate ownership since 1936, was demolished, while the automotive production facilities were heavily damaged. With so much destruction, the new owners postponed plans to sell off the remaining assets. German bombers would return again over the next two years, causing even more damage, but one of the greatest losses came when Healey departed for the Rootes Group, where he worked on armoured car development.

Despite his departure, Healey remained in contact with his former colleagues at Triumph, hoping to return after the war to build a sports car design that he had been working on in his spare time. In late 1944, Healey presented his plan to the management at Wards, who initially seemed receptive to the proposal. After some consideration, however, the project was rejected on the grounds that Healey lacked sufficient manufacturing experience, which seemed curious considering that he had already served the company in several executive capacities.

Having rejected Healey, Wards set out to find a buyer for the damaged factories and the Triumph name, which were the only valuable assets that remained. Of the potential candidates, Ford and Vauxhall were quickly dismissed, while Austin and Nuffield were considered too large to bother with the shambles that remained. The remaining possibilities were the Standard Motor Company that Bettmann had once helped to save before the First World War, and the Rootes Group, which already owned Hillman, Humber, Sunbeam and Talbot.

In the three decades since Bettmann's brief involvement, Standard had prospered building sensible family automobiles and providing components for smaller manufacturers such as Morgan and Swallow to use in their own products. Much of the success that the company had achieved could be credited to Sir John Black, who had become managing director in 1933. Under his leadership, Standard was an early proponent of the wartime shadow factory

Standard made its reputation on highly regarded saloons such as the 1939 Flying Standard Twelve de Luxe saloon seen here, but Sir John Black wanted to build more sporting models, leading Standard to purchase Triumph in 1944. (Magic Car Pics)

programme and had plans in place to resume civilian production well before the competition, which was still focused on building munitions.

Under New Ownership

Despite a mercurial personality and troublesome reputation, Black was a visionary who hoped that Triumph's prewar reputation for performance and engineering excellence could contribute to his burgeoning automotive empire. Better yet, Triumph's sports car experience might help him compete with SS-Jaguar's Sir William Lyons, who had considerable success building affordable sporting models in the late 1930s.

With such benefits in mind, Standard purchased Triumph on 24 November 1944, and held its first board meeting less than a month before the war ended in Europe. Not long afterwards, Black also reached an agreement with Harry Ferguson to manufacture light tractors at the former shadow factory at Banner Lane. More importantly, he also convinced the tractor magnate to allow the use of a new engine under development at Standard.

Standard's first postwar model was the Vanguard, powered by a modified version of the engine used in the Ferguson tractor. With contemporary styling and good performance, it was an immediate hit with customers around the world, especially in traditional export markets. But notwithstanding the Vanguard's success, Black wanted the same for Triumph, starting with two models, a saloon and a touring roadster. Both would benefit from experience gained building aircraft during the war, relying on tube frames and aluminium bodywork, but with little money available it had to incorporate many existing Standard components to reduce costs.

It was no secret that Black badly wanted a proper sports car to serve as a flagship for his growing operation, explaining his personal involvement in the touring roadster's development. Despite an aluminium body, however, the Triumph 1800 Roadster was rather heavy and boasted curious styling, an amalgam of anachronistic design cues and odd features like a dickey seat in the boot. A poor seller from the start, it never gained traction in the market, even after the larger Vanguard engine appeared in 1949.

Refusing to abandon his pursuit of a proper sports car, Black asked Walter Belgrove, Triumph's design chief, to fashion a more modern and compelling shape. The TRX appeared at the 1950 Paris Auto Salon, appearing rather futuristic with an envelope-style streamlined body. A bold effort, the TRX was too complex and expensive to produce in mass quantities, forcing Triumph to return to the drawing board.

With both MG and Jaguar experiencing great success on the export market, Black became impatient, demanding a design that could sell in the United States. While Black might have wanted to take on Lyons, Abingdon's T-series was an easier target. It was also much cheaper to build an affordable sports car, particularly since Jaguar's XK120 was a new design while the TD was really a prewar platform in disguise.

When the 20TS appeared at the London Motor Show in 1952, Black finally had the sports car that he desired. Although criticised for poor handling and dubious styling, it showed obvious potential, which was fully realised when the original design was hastily revised to create the TR2. With a rugged frame and brisk performance from the Vanguard-derived 1,991cc engine, Triumph's new sports car was more powerful and modern than the MG and could even effectively challenge the more expensive Austin-Healey 100 (which had debuted at Earls Court alongside the 20TS).

Notwithstanding strong market competition, the initial TR model sold well after a slow start, cementing Triumph's reputation with motoring enthusiasts and allowing the firm to stand in the front rank of the world's sports car manufacturers. By the time that the TR3 appeared in 1957, Austin-Healey, MG and Triumph found themselves competing for many of the same customers, each with one modern sports car model for sale, all priced within a few hundred pounds of one another. That dynamic changed, however, when Austin-Healey's Sprite arrived the following year, representing an entirely new sports car option for consumers at a price that significantly undercut the existing vehicles on the market. The Sprite proved an immediate hit with customers on both sides of the Atlantic and produced strong profits for BMC, but it also showed the rest of the industry that an opportunity existed at the bottom end of the market, particularly in North America, forcing them to scramble to field a viable competitor.

The Triumph 20TS debuted at the 1952 London Motor Show and served as the basis for a successful line of TR sports cars following hasty revisions to improve its appearance and performance. (Graham Robson Collection)

Chapter 2
Birth of the Bomb

While Donald and Geoffrey Healey had laid out the Sprite's novel design from scratch around readily sourced mechanical bits from the parts bin at BMC, Triumph travelled an easier road since an ideal platform for a small sports car had recently arrived in the form of the Herald.

Triumph had first considered plans for a new small car in 1956 to replace the existing Eights and Tens, but concerns over sourcing the bodies in satisfactory numbers, and determining the technical and aesthetic parameters for the cars, slowed down the process. The styling issue was particularly problematic, especially since Walter Belgrove had resigned the previous fall after almost thirty years on the job, unhappy that outside stylists had started to encroach upon what had once been his exclusive domain.

With more time to ponder the parameters of the small car project, Managing Director Alick Dick, who had assumed control after Sir John Black was forced out two years earlier, and General Manager Martin Tustin decided to abandon thoughts of monocoque construction and focus their efforts on a vehicle that would require minimal capital investment for tooling and encompass an entire range of variants, including a saloon, coupé, convertible, van and estate, all built upon a separate chassis that could be easily assembled in various overseas facilities as Completely Knocked Down (CKD) kits in former colonies such as Australia, India and South Africa.

There are few differences between the Spitfire in final production form and the Bomb prototype that had arrived at Canley in 1960. Note the different grille design, lower placement of the door handles, and badging on the leading edge of the bonnet.

13

An Italian Job

For the first half of 1957, various styling proposals for the small car project were considered and then dismissed, Webster even denouncing one candidate that had been presented as 'a mechanical bathtub on wheels.' With Belgrove no longer around, fate intervened in the guise of Giovanni Michelotti. The young Italian had been hard at work around this time on a private commission for Captain Raymond Flowers, who was attempting to manufacture an automobile in Egypt, built around an affordable vehicle named the Frisky. In an offhand remark to Harry Webster, Triumph's engineering director, Flowers boasted that he had secured the services of a talented designer who could build a finished prototype in less than ninety days, and do so for a reasonable fee.

Triumph's executives were eager to meet the unidentified stylist, but Flowers demanded to act as an intermediary, allowing him to maintain strict control over his discovery. After some enterprising detective work from Webster and Tustin, the pair uncovered the name of the heretofore anonymous stylist and found out that the young Italian had already earned a reputation as a blossoming genius, being surprised that Flowers had characterised Michelotti's talents without embellishment. Although still in his thirties, Michelotti had amassed an impressive portfolio, having worked with notable coachbuilders such as Allemano, Bertone, Ghia and Vignale.

Michelotti had learned his trade as an apprentice with Stabilimenti Farina while still a young teenager, before the war put his career on hold. By 1949, he had established his own design house, working on a commission basis for larger firms. He soon cultivated a close relationship with Carrozzeria Vignale, working with them on several permutations of the Ferrari 166, 212, 225, 250 and 340. Significantly, he also had some experience working with British sports cars, having penned bespoke coachwork for various Austin-Healeys and MGs for Switzerland's Ghia-Aigle, allowing him to become familiar with their construction and getting a feel for their smaller proportions compared to the larger Italian machinery that had been his bread and butter.

Hark the Herald

Michelotti's first assignment for Triumph was really along the lines of an audition, styling a TR3-based 'dream car' to determine if the existing platform could serve as the basis for an entirely new vehicle. Almost alone among his vast portfolio, his effort was overly gimmicky and unattractive, resembling a smaller Ford Thunderbird and featuring gauche styling elements such as a massive grille, sharp tail fins, and duotone livery. Nonetheless, it attracted attention, cost only £3,000 to build and arrived on time, all factors which endeared him to the executives at Canley.

Final appearances aside, it had been a successful trial, and Michelotti was immediately offered an informal arrangement to work on several upcoming projects, including Project Zobo, which was the name given to the small car project. It was his outstanding work on the latter commission that cemented Michelotti's relationship with Triumph. Working with Harry Webster at his Turin base, the

An amazingly versatile platform, the Herald was offered in a number of variants, including the popular convertible and a practical wagon called the Estate. A van known as the Courier was also available. (Magic Car Pics)

small car's final design was sketched out during a single evening, and the three prototypes in coupé, saloon and estate versions were completed for the incredibly low price of £10,000, made possible due to his strong relationship with Vignale.

By the time that the Zobo program spawned the Herald in 1959, the Sprite had already established a successful niche in North America. Keen to enter the fray as soon as possible, Triumph considered putting forward the Herald Coupé as its small sports car candidate. Although the Herald was more technically advanced than the Sprite, featuring an independent rear suspension and rack and pinion steering, Michelotti felt that it lacked the necessary sporting appearance to pose a challenge to the small Austin-Healey roadster.

Without prompting from Canley, Michelotti penned a more sporting alternative that used the Herald's mechanical bits but with a shorter wheelbase. Alick Dick, Triumph's Managing Director, recalled how the designer worked: 'Michelotti was always reeling off new designs; you just couldn't stop him. If you took him out to dinner he'd get practically every menu card in the place, design a car, and leave them as souvenirs for the waiters! He could design a car in four or five minutes, and the nice thing was that he would do it to our ideas, not just his own.'

The preliminary sketches were favourably received, allowing Technical Chief Harry Webster to submit a formal proposal to the Standard-Triumph board in April 1960, which granted approval to pursue the design's development. Assigned the code name Bomb, it was to use existing Herald mechanical components to hold down the costs, and be fitted with a fiberglass or steel body. Webster immediately directed Michelotti to expand on his initial ideas: 'He would submit five or six in the space of four or five days, then George (Turnbull) and I would choose the line we liked most and we'd invited Michelotti to make a complete design and prototype.'

Although the board did not formally approve an actual mock-up until September 1960, Webster had already sent a 948cc Herald Coupé to Michelotti in Turin for conversion into the prototype Bomb. Known for his incredibly fast working pace, the Italian designer immediately removed the

Harry Webster behind the wheel of a Triumph Herald rolling chassis at the Canley works. The Herald's engine and gearbox were both derived from the units installed in the Standard Ten. (Magic Car Pics)

An early design sketch for Michelotti's Bomb, displaying numerous styling themes seen in far more expensive contemporary Italian sports cars. Arguably, one of the Italian virtuoso's most attractive efforts, this effort would result in the production Spitfire. (Edgardo Michelotti and Giancarlo Cavallini)

As the design evolved, the Bomb adopted more conventional elements, abandoning the diminutive bumperettes, raked prow, frameless upper windscreen and prominent bonnet bulge. (Edgardo Michelotti and Giancarlo Cavallini)

Herald's bodywork and shortened the chassis frame at Webster's insistence to obtain an 83-inch wheelbase. Michelotti then penned an entirely new curvaceous shape for the small sports car, but retained the innovative one-piece front end assembly that made the Herald so simple to service and repair. Incredibly, it took less than two weeks to construct a wooden buck and fabricate the external panels, allowing the attractive little roadster to depart for England in October.

A Michelotti rendering contemplating the vehicle's competition future, depicting a left-hand drive model on an Alpine rally course. One of history's most talented and prolific automotive designers, Michelotti often produced renderings depicting styling proposals in their natural environment. (Edgardo Michelotti and Giancarlo Cavallini)

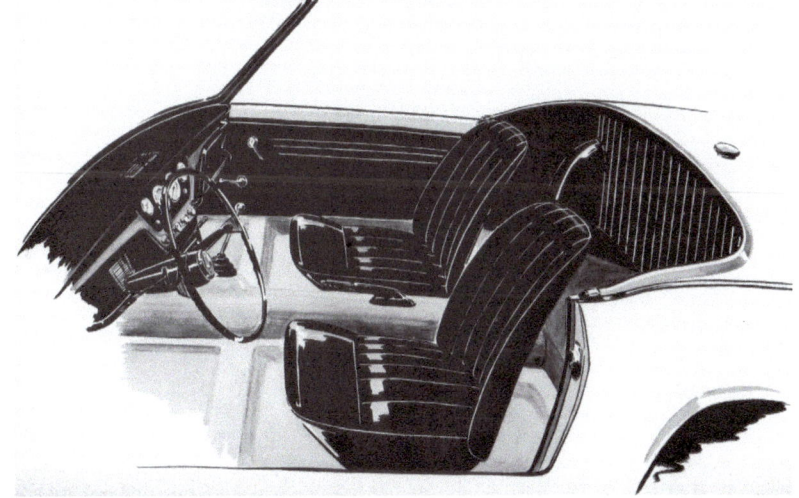

A Michelotti sketch showing the Spitfire interior in almost its final form. Note the central instrument binnacle adopted to reduce production costs and the handsome bucket seats. (Edgardo Michelotti and Giancarlo Cavallini)

Lost and Found

The Bomb's arrival in Coventry, however, could not have been more poorly timed. Throughout that summer American sales had slowed considerably, including the best-selling TR3A, which had been overproduced due to poor forecasting. In the United Kingdom, an economic recession had restricted available credit, causing demand for new automobiles to dwindle, and without a significant capital reserve, Triumph was in dire financial straits. Making matters worse, warranty claims for the initial batch of Heralds were much higher than expected, and the company needed the available cash on hand to pay for factory construction and new production tooling. With no resources to support further development work, Michelotti's beautiful Bomb was tucked away in the the Experimental Department, placed under a cover, and then forgotten.

Meanwhile, Triumph was casting about for merger candidates that could provide the necessary funds to allow the firm to weather the current financial storm. After discussions with Rover failed, Leyland, which had been wanting to expand its business operations for some time, stepped in to save the day on 5 December 1960, although the merger was not formally announced until the following spring. To stem the massive losses that Triumph continued to suffer (about £600,000 every month), Leyland management suspended all of Triumph's pending capital projects, delaying the TR4's launch.

As described by Leyland's Lord Stokes: 'It was complete chaos – and they spent money like water. It was unbelievable. Everybody had a company car – all the secretaries, the assistant secretaries, the wives, and everybody else. We soon stopped that. The culture was completely different: when I was in charge of the trolleybuses at Leyland, I was sent out to sell them because I had a motorbike. I was sent on my motorbike because it saved money.'

Stanley Markland, who soon replaced Alick Dick as Standard-Triumph's Managing Director, became the liaison between the two companies during the transition. As described by Harry Webster, his arrival was met with trepidation: 'Everyone thought he would be a hatchet man – he had been one with other

The original Bomb prototype was constructed on a shortened Herald chassis frame and reached the market fundamentally unaltered, save for taller doors to accommodate the winding windows and the addition of lettering and trim for the bonnet and boot lids. (Graham Robson Collection)

companies he had run – but he never did this with us at Triumph.' Although anxious to reduce expenses, Markland also took a strong interest in the manufacturing side of the ledger, befitting his engineering background. During his first few months at Canley, he conducted frequent inspection tours, often accompanied by Webster, who recalled the moment when the new executive encountered the Bomb for the first time:

> One day as we walked through the warehouses at the factory with Stanley Markland we came upon a dusty canvas. "What is this?" asked Stanley who wanted to uncover the sheet. I removed it and when he saw "the Bomb" he exclaimed: "It's amazing – no more, no less. But how it could it have been forgotten?" So I told him that it was a working prototype, and it was much more than a formal effort. What happened next I will never forget. He looked at me, got in the car, started the engine, and took a tour through the warehouse. When he came back, he astonishedly told me: "It's very good and we'll manufacture it."

The Bomb Takes Flight

Markland kept his promise, the decision made much easier by the appearance of an improved Sprite, along with an identical sibling in the form of the MG Midget, only weeks after the Bomb's impromptu test drive. Formal approval to proceed was issued on 13 July 1961, even though Harry Webster had already started work prior to receiving the word, confident of management's final decision. Thankfully, the external styling was almost perfect, requiring only an increase in the door's height to accommodate the winding windows, which neither the Sprite nor the Midget possessed, and a revised dash arrangement suitable for use with both left- and right-hand drive applications. On the other hand, the chassis, suspension and running gear would all need modification, requiring several months of effort to address.

With Triumph having no previous experience with fiberglass bodywork, with the exception of the TR3S and TRS racers, management made the prudent decision to use pressed steel shells and assigned the work to the Forward Radiator Company. Due to numerous complaints about the Herald's shakes and rattles, resulting from the manner in which the small car was bolted together, Triumph decided to spot-weld the production Bombs, brazed as necessary, to increase the structural integrity of the entire body assembly. Clever incorporation of unitary construction principles, along with rugged box section sills, snugly contoured floor pressings and a strong internal structure, combined to produce an extremely rigid bodyshell, eliminating most of the flexure associated with traditional body-on-frame designs. As in the Herald, a single forward-hinged hood provided unparalleled access to the engine, making service and maintenance simpler to accomplish.

Although Michelotti's Bomb had been built on a standard Herald chassis, shortened to provide an 83-inch wheelbase, Triumph's engineers decided to modify the chassis, resulting in a substantial backbone frame. Both ends of the main longitudinal frame rails were made wider to accommodate the engine and

While not very practical, this image emphasizes the fact that the Spitfire featured an opening boot lid, which is something that the original Sprite never offered. (Graham Robson Collection)

front suspension at one end, and the rear suspension and differential assembly at the other. In order to eliminate the Herald's outriggers and side rails, the bodyshell incorporated robust sills and the entire structure benefitted from substantial reinforcement throughout, keeping the weight at around 150 lbs.

The Herald's front and rear suspension assemblies were incorporated with minimal modification, except that the locating radius arms for the swing-axle independent rear suspension were mounted on the body rather than the chassis crossmember and an antiroll bar was installed at the front end. Retention of the Herald's rack and pinion steering unit resulted in an incredible 24-foot turning circle – a feat that few vehicles could match. In order to show up the competition from Abingdon, which relied on four-wheel drum brakes, front disc brakes were made standard equipment – another important selling feature that would help entice potential customers.

It was also clear that more power was needed under the bonnet to compete against the Sprite and Midget, resulting in the abandonment of the Bomb's 948cc four-cylinder engine for the larger 1,147cc unit from the Herald 1200. The increased displacement came from an enlarged 69.3 mm bore that was made possible by incorporating a slight desaxé to the cylinder alignment, providing the necessary room in the block for the larger pistons. To further boost the unit's output past the 41 bhp available in the Herald 1200, twin SU HS2 carburettors were fitted, along with an elevated compression ratio, hotter camshaft, larger inlet and exhaust valves, and a less restrictive exhaust manifold. The modifications resulted in 63 bhp at 5,750 rpm and 67 pound-feet of torque at 3,500 rpm – enough to propel the small sports car from 0 to 60 mph in 15.4 seconds and allow it to reach a top speed of more than 90 mph, which was a substantial advantage over the Austin-Healey Sprite Mk II's 19.6 seconds and 84.6 mph.

By the following spring, John Lloyd's engineering staff were hard at work testing the first two prototypes built at Canley, constantly tweaking the design as necessary to achieve the desired dynamic performance and reliability, but always aware that volume production was set to begin soon. Handling refinements consumed much of the time, requiring different spring and damper combinations to find the right balance. Maintaining the correct camber for swing axle rear assembly required tyre pressures of 18 psi at the front and 24 psi at the rear – a startling differential intended to induce understeer in most cornering situations.

Although sharing the same powerplant as the Herald, the 1,147cc engine in the Spitfire produced 63 bhp at 5,750 rpm and 67 pound-feet of torque at 3,500 rpm through the addition of twin SU HS2 1¼-inch carburettors and an increased 9:1 compression ratio. The available power made it possible to reach a 91 mph top speed and record the run from 0 to 60 mph in 15.4 seconds. Note that the remote header tank leading aft from the radiator should be painted in a gold tone finish.

The boot offers generous space for luggage and tools – much more than was available in most contemporary rivals. Note that the petrol tank is located behind the forward hardboard panel and the spare tyre and wheel are affixed to a bracket welded to the boot floor.

The script on the boot lid denotes the presence of overdrive in this attractive example finished in Wedgewood Blue. An option that was never available in the rival Sprite, the Laycock de Normanville unit allowed the Spitfire to comfortably reach motorway cruising speeds without excessive thrashing of the small displacement engine.

At a time when many affordable automobiles were fitted with minimal instrumentation, the Spitfire boasted a fairly comprehensive array of gauges. As seen in this image, the instruments were contained in a central binnacle that could facilitate use in both left- and right-hand drive markets without alteration on the production line.

In sharp contrast to the austere Sprite and Midget twins from the BMC stable, the Spitfire benefitted from rather more luxurious interior appointments, including superior upholstery, comprehensive carpeting, contoured seatbacks and plenty of storage under the dash and behind the seats.

While the Sprite and Midget had to make do without winding windows until 1964, the Spitfire had them from the beginning, along with full door cards that made the interior seem slightly narrower than in its BMC rivals.

A Sparkling Debut

Despite Webster's wish to retain the original moniker, the Bomb became the Spitfire later that summer as an homage to Supermarine's fabled fighter that had dominated the skies during the Battle of Britain. As the production line at Canley built the first batch of production examples, the Spitfire 4 debuted at the London Motor Show on 17 October 1962. From the moment that the doors opened at Earls Court, the car received an enthusiastic reception from the public and the press, who were impressed with its styling, performance and comprehensive kit, particularly the independent rear suspension and disc brakes, features that were unavailable in most sports cars, much less one sold at such an affordable price.

Despite some criticism of the Spitfire's narrow cabin and the engine's lack of refinement, *The Motor*'s overall conclusion was rather complimentary: 'A sports car of great merit, the Triumph Spitfire will appeal equally as a comfortable road car and useful competition mount.' *Autosport* was even more laudatory, stating that: 'This is a fast sports car that has perfect town manners and an appearance that will break down the resistance of many prospective owners.' Despite strong demand, especially from overseas, only 1,289 examples were built before the year's end, forcing customers who had already placed orders to wait weeks or months for delivery. Stung by the Herald's premature introduction and the warranty claims that ensued, Triumph had resolved to reserve the initial batch of production vehicles for sale in the United Kingdom, where any problems that arose could be more easily addressed directly at the factory.

This decision created exasperation in the United States, where enthusiasts had read the positive reviews in the motoring press and were eager to see the Spitfire for themselves. As Michael Cook, Triumph's American public relations manager, recalled: 'The dealers raved about the new car. They knew value when they saw it, and they also knew that the MG Midget/Austin-Healey Sprite twins were no match for it.' Throughout the first months of 1963, Spitfires crossed the Atlantic in increasing numbers, sparking a 30 per cent increase in Standard-Triumph's overall sales.

The Triumph Spitfire was officially introduced at the 1962 London Motor Show at Earls Court, where it featured prominently alongside the TR4 and Herald. (Graham Robson Collection)

The only significant criticism levied against the Spitfire was the disconcerting tendency of the rear wheels to tuck under during aggressive cornering, causing the rear end to lose adhesion. This was not an issue under normal driving conditions, as *Road & Track* considered the handling 'better at touring speeds than others in the same class'. Nevertheless, camber compensators, similar to those used on the Volkswagen Beetle, were soon available from dealers to limit rear wheel travel, which reduced the problem to a great extent.

A Standard-Triumph promotional image featuring an export model with R. W. 'Kas' Kastner at the wheel. (Plain English Archive)

The split grille adopted the same pattern as the contemporary Vitesse 1600. Note the use of shorter and thicker overriders than in the Bomb prototype, the use of bonnet lettering and a badge similar to those fitted to the TR4.

Giovanni Michelotti's timeless design originally reached the market as the Spitfire 4 to emphasise the powerplant under the bonnet. It was retrospectively known as the Mk I to distinguish it from the Mk II that followed.

With Triumph's lean period at the beginning of the decade fading fast in the rear view mirror, its goal was to increase its share of the American market, being eager to capitalise on what most experts considered the most complete line of sports cars in the market. As *Time* magazine recognized: 'If anything can accelerate Standard-Triumph's progress, the Spitfire ought to be it.' With such strong sales, there was little need or incentive to modify the car much during

Despite its simplicity, the Spitfire's erect-it-yourself hood provided best in class weather protection. When not in use the hood frame resided behind a panel at the front of the boot while the PVC hood was stowed separately after careful folding to prevent creasing the quarter windows and backlight. The hood could also be placed in a special pouch to protect it from damage.

The bisected rear bumpers with attached overriders offered adequate protection from damage incurred in parking incidents and were more attractive than the full-width alternative. Note the centrally located petrol filler cap similar to the one used on the TR4 and the fact that this example is missing the 'Triumph' lettering that should run across the boot lid above the handle.

The Spitfire retains its attractive lines even with the hood raised. Most examples were fitted with 13 x 3½-inch pressed steel wheels and simple chrome hub caps rather than the non-standard chrome wire wheels seen here. Wheel covers from the Vitesse 1600 were also available at extra cost while the optional wire wheels would have been finished with silver paint.

its initial production run, with the running changes limited to minor details like split-skirt pistons, side panels for the engine compartment to promote better cooling, and elimination of the remote radiator header tank. A Laycock de Normanville D-type electrical overdrive became an option in October 1963, a feature totally unavailable in Abingdon's Sprite and Midget, followed the following year by an attractive hardtop and wire wheels.

Spitfire 4 (1962–1965)

Engine:

Four cylinders in line. Cast-iron block and cylinder head.

Capacity:	1,147cc
Bore x Stroke:	69.3 mm x 76 mm
Valve Actuation:	Pushrod with overhead valves
Compression Ratio:	9.0:1
Carburettors:	2 x SU HS2
Output:	63 bhp at 5,750 rpm
	67 pound-feet at 3,500 rpm

Transmission:

Rear-wheel drive. Four-speed gearbox with synchromesh on the three upper gears. Electric overdrive optional from early 1963.

Suspension:

Front: Independent front suspension with coil springs and wishbones. Antiroll bar. Telescopic dampers.

Rear: Independent rear suspension with transverse leaf spring and swing axles. Telescopic dampers. Location by radius arms.

Steering:

Rack and pinion.

Brakes:

Front disc and rear drums.

Rolling Stock:

13-inch pressed steel or wire wheels. 5.20 x 13-inch tyres.

Bodywork:

Separate chassis with steel panels.

Dimensions:

Length:	12 ft 1 in.
Wheelbase:	6 ft 11 in.
Front Track:	4 ft 1 in.
Rear Track:	4 ft 0 in.
Width:	4 ft 9 in.
Height:	3 ft 11½ in.
Kerb Weight:	14.25 cwt

Performance:

Maximum Speed:	91 mph
0 to 60 mph:	15.4 sec
Standing ¼ mile:	19.5 sec

Production:

45,753

By December 1964, when the time came to introduce a freshened model, 45,753 Spitfire 4s had been produced, making Triumph the most successful manufacturer of sporting cars in England. It outsold the Sprite and Midget by a wide margin and was proving effective at attracting new buyers, including a significant number of women, into the sports car fold.

Given the continued demand for the original version, the Spitfire Mk II incorporated only modest changes. Externally, the car remained the same, except for a new grille, but the cabin became far more luxurious, with vinyl trim covering the previously painted interior surfaces, new seat cushions, optional leather trim and moulded carpet in place of the rubber floor mats. Inside the engine compartment, a new camshaft with more overlap and higher lift, along with a tubular extractor exhaust manifold, boosted power to 67 bhp at 6,000 rpm. A 6.5-inch diameter Borg & Beck diaphragm spring clutch replaced the Bellville spring washer unit used in the Spitfire 4, improving clutch feel and increasing reliability in competition use. For those interested in more performance, Triumph dealers offered three staged tuning kits, created with the input of the increasingly successful North American Competition Department, which operated under R. W. (Kas) Kastner's supervision in California.

Pitched Battle

The Spitfire Mk II arrived alongside the TR4A in March 1965 and both continued to sell well, despite not insignificant price increases and increasing competition from BMC. While the Austin-Healey 3000 and MGB presented a formidable challenge for the TR, the Sprite and Midget seemed to always be one step behind the little Triumph, having been forced to add more powerful engines, disc brakes and winding windows just to maintain the pace. In every year since the Spitfire had arrived it had outsold the Abingdon twins – a trend that Triumph wanted to continue well into the future.

While most of the American motoring press continued to praise the car at the same time that fault was found with the vehicle's tendency to tuck in the rear wheels during hard cornering, not everyone agreed, particularly at home. 'The Spitfire clings to the road better than any Triumph we have driven,' wrote *Autocar*. 'On a dry test track at the very giddy (and rapid) limit of adhesion, the tail breaks away in the customary swing-axle fashion, but by then most owners would have backed off, thinking the car would never unstick.'

Over the three years of the Mk II's production, running improvements were limited to the addition of camshaft bearings, a modified cylinder head for better cooling of the exhaust ports, new oil seals, revised dampers and minor trim modifications, validating the excellence of the original package. Customers continued to flock to Triumph dealers, despite the fact that most of the claimants to the Spitfire's throne were less expensive.

With a clear sales advantage over the Sprite and Midget there was little need to change the basic formula when the Spitfire Mk II arrived in December 1964. Almost identical in external appearance to its predecessor, the new model introduced more luxurious interior appointments and a modest gain in performance.

With the same visual identity as the Spitfire 4 Mk I, it is difficult to distinguish between the two models. Early examples were fitted with the same lever-type door handles, but later vehicles such as this 1966 variant featured more robust fixed units that operated with the push of a button. Note the standard road wheels and hub caps that differed only in minor details from those fitted to the previous edition.

Black vinyl trim graced the previously painted metal surfaces while more comprehensive carpeting was used throughout the cabin. This late example features the three-spoke steering wheel that replaced the earlier Herald-type wheel seen in the Mk I. Although retaining the same frame assemblies, the seats offered more padding to increase their comfort.

When *Car and Driver* announced that the Spitfire had been named the 'Best GT/Sports Car Under $2500' in a widely publicised reader poll, the American magazine remarked: 'Maybe it's the independent rear suspension, maybe it's the slightly better performance than its rivals, but for some reason or another, the Triumph Spitfire was a clear-cut choice for honors ... it won with surprising ease over the Austin-Healey Sprites, receiving 32.3 per cent of the vote while its rival polled 20.4 per cent. Many automotive journalists tend to lump cars in this class together, reasoning that the price, quality and performance of the Spitfire, Sprite, Morgan 4/4 and the MG Midget are so similar that one can only make a subjective choice. You the readers must disagree.'

The most significant threat to the Spitfire's continued dominance came from American lawmakers rather than rival manufacturers, since the tide was beginning to turn in the world's most important sports car market. The release of consumer advocate Ralph Nader's tirade against the automobile entitled *Unsafe at Any Speed* resulted in several new rules directed at improving automotive safety at the same time that new anti-pollution standards were set to arrive. Thankfully, work was already underway at Canley to meet these challenges, resulting in the third iteration of Triumph's small sports car champion.

Spitfire Mk 2 (1965–1967)

Engine:

Four cylinders in line. Cast-iron block and cylinder head.

Capacity:	1,147cc
Bore x Stroke:	69.3 mm x 76 mm
Valve Actuation:	Pushrod with overhead valves
Compression Ratio:	9.0:1
Carburettors:	2 x SU HS2
Output:	67 bhp at 6,000 rpm
	67 pound-feet at 3,750 rpm

Transmission:

Rear-wheel drive. Four-speed gearbox with synchromesh on the three upper gears. Electric overdrive optional.

Suspension:

Front: Independent front suspension with coil springs and wishbones. Antiroll bar. Telescopic dampers.

Rear: Independent rear suspension with transverse leaf spring and swing axles. Telescopic dampers. Location by radius arms.

Steering:

Rack and pinion.

Brakes:

Front disc and rear drums.

Rolling Stock:

13-inch pressed steel or wire wheels. 5.20 x 13-inch tyres.

Bodywork:

Separate chassis with steel panels.

Dimensions:

Length:	12 ft 1 in.
Wheelbase:	6 ft 11 in.
Front Track:	4 ft 1 in.
Rear Track:	4 ft 0 in.
Width:	4 ft 9 in.
Height:	3 ft 11½ in.
Kerb Weight:	14.25 cwt

Performance:

Maximum Speed:	92 mph
0 to 60 mph:	15.0 sec.
Standing ¼ mile:	20.4 sec.

Production:

37,409

The instrumentation layout remained unchanged though the warning bands on the rev counter were changed with the addition of a second colour and the face of the water temperature gauge was altered slightly with the inclusion of a red and blue to indicate the hot and cold extremes.

In many ways, the Spitfire was more technically advanced than the more expensive TR4 with an independent rear suspension and some primitive monocoque construction techniques. Although both models featured Michelotti styling, other than the shared windscreen frame and handsome lines there were few styling elements in common between the two siblings.

The pressed steel wheels and hub caps carried over from the Mk I with the rest of the front end details remaining unchanged in the Mk II.

The fact that the Spitfire boasted an independent rear suspension was not touted on the boot lid as it was in the TR4A. This seems strange given that the Spitfire was the most affordable British sports car to have this feature, allowing it to benefit from excellent handling under most commonly encountered conditions.

The pressed steel wheels were fitted with 3.5-inch-wide tyres while examples ordered with the optional wire wheels had tyres that were an inch wider, increasing the available grip considerably. This particular vehicle has been fitted with modern radial tyres that are wider than the original cross-ply items.

Chapter 3
Under Pressure

With more than three out of every four Spitfires sold in North America, there was little question that the model would be modified to comply with the safety and emissions standards that were about to come into effect. The Spitfire Mk III that appeared at the Geneva Auto Salon in March 1967 not only responded to the new mandates, but also raised the stakes against the Sprite and Midget, which had received larger 1.3-litre engines the previous fall.

The most obvious differences from the previous model were external, with the front bumper raised 9 inches to satisfy American height requirements and the rear quarter bumpers elevated to a position directly under the taillights, necessitating the elimination of the attendant overriders. For more convenient and effective weather protection, a fully convertible hood replaced the 'erector-set' assembly that had been time-consuming to raise in the rain, while the interior benefitted from a better selection of upholstery colours, a new 15-inch steering wheel and walnut trim on the instrument panel, which made the Spitfire seem more luxurious in a single stroke.

The most significant change, however, resulted from the installation of the 1,296cc engine that had debuted in the 1300 saloon. For use in the Mk III, however, a new eight-port cylinder head was utilised with more efficient combustion chambers, breathing through a new inlet and exhaust manifolds. The larger powerplant produced 75 bhp at 6,000 rpm and 75 pound-feet of torque at 4,000 rpm – enough to reduce the time needed to sprint from 0 to 60 mph to 14.5 seconds and increase the top speed to 95 mph. With the increased performance on

Despite continued strong sales, Triumph installed a larger capacity engine under the bonnet of their small sports car to stay ahead of the competition. The change occasioned the arrival of the Mk III in March 1967, which also heralded the first meaningful visual change since the first Spitfire had appeared five years earlier.

hand, a more robust clutch and stiffer springs were installed, along with uprated Girling 14 LF brake callipers that featured thicker pads for longer life and reduced fade after repeated use.

The only other revisions of note were a negative ground electrical system, anti-burst door locks and revised auxiliary lights. With more power and better weather protection, an already attractive vehicle was made even more so, and sales continued to exceed expectations. 'The best reason for buying a Spitfire is that the thing is a ball to drive,' explained *Car and Driver* in assessing the model's merits. 'Everyone starts out with a Spitfire, or something similar, and we don't know anyone who looks back at the experience with anything other than great fondness. It is all a necessary part of being led into the car game. You go from some vast, floaty sedan – with umpteen turns of free lash in the steering – into a jouncy, feisty little item like the Spitfire. It is confined and harsh of ride beyond all reason, and you love it. You won't be able to explain it all to your friends, but they will understand, dimly, that it's about fun, and young manhood found or rediscovered. So Walter Mitty pulls on his driving gloves and is soon hurtling through Arnage, or cranking around the hairpin at Stavelot. Man does not live by comfort alone. Perhaps there is some danger that cars may become too good to be interesting, or maybe just too good to be fun. Triumph's Spitfire Mk III has not yet fallen into that characterless condition.'

Although the GT6 received an improved rear suspension in late 1968, rectifying the problems associated with the original swing axle arrangement, the Spitfire soldiered on unaltered. 'Although we have no wish to malign the reputation of this very pleasant sports car,' wrote *Autocar*, 'we make no apology for referring to its handling limitations. Its stablemates, the GT6 and Vitesse, now have a completely redesigned rear suspension system. What a pity that the Spitfire has not been included.'

Seen from the front, the Mk III appears to be a new design, but the profile remained the same since the external panels remained unaltered, except for some slight bonnet alterations to accommodate the higher front bumper assembly.

The Spitfire's 1,296cc engine had already proven itself for more than two years in the 1300 saloon and was essentially a 1,147cc unit modified with a larger 73.7 mm bore. Although the camshaft from the Mk II was retained, a vastly improved eight-port cylinder head was fitted to replace the siamesed inlet ports used in the previous powerplant.

Although the horsepower in the Mk III had increased only a slight amount to 70 bhp at 6,000 rpm, the available torque received a significant boost to 75 pound-feet at 4,000 rpm. When fitted with the optional electric overdrive, the Spitfire's third iteration could almost match the high-speed cruising capabilities of the much larger and more expensive MGB and TR4. Other than the high-performance renewable air filters and ribbed aluminium valve cover, the engine compartment is otherwise in standard trim.

The Mk III's seats and door cards were carried over from before, but were available in a wider range of colours. The most significant change, however, was the arrival of a true convertible hood to replace the 'erect-it-yourself' assembly used previously.

Spitfire Mk 3 (1967–1970)

Engine:

Four cylinders in line. Cast-iron block and cylinder head.

Capacity:	1,296 cc
Bore x Stroke:	73.7 mm x 76 mm
Valve Actuation:	Pushrod with overhead valves
Compression Ratio:	9.0:1
	8.5:1 (US:1969–70)
Carburettors:	2 x SU HS2
Output:	75 bhp at 6,000 rpm
	68 bhp at 5,500 rpm (US: 1969–70)
	75 pound-feet at 4,000 rpm
	73 pound-feet at 3,000 rpm (US: 1969–70)

Transmission:

Rear-wheel drive. Four-speed gearbox with synchromesh on the three upper gears. Electric overdrive optional.

Suspension:

Front: Independent front suspension with coil springs and wishbones. Antiroll bar. Telescopic dampers.

Rear: Independent rear suspension with transverse leaf spring and swing axles. Telescopic dampers. Location by radius arms.

Steering:

Rack and pinion.

Brakes:

Front disc and rear drums.

Rolling Stock:

13-inch pressed steel or wire wheels. 5.20 x 13-inch tyres.

Bodywork:

Separate chassis with steel panels.

Dimensions:

Length:	12 ft 1 in.
Wheelbase:	6 ft 11 in.
Front Track:	4 ft 1 in.
Rear Track:	4 ft 0 in.
Width:	4 ft 9 in.
Height:	3 ft 11½ in.
Kerb Weight:	15.5 cwt

Performance:

Maximum Speed:	95 mph
0 to 60 mph:	14.5 sec.
Standing ¼ mile:	19.6 sec.

Production:

65,320

The Mk III received wood veneer trim for the central instrument binnacle, matching the look in other models in the Triumph family. This example is fitted with the rare wood-trimmed Formula steering wheel that was available for an additional £7 10s. The additional instruments are non-standard items.

Potential customers were beginning to take note of the criticism, with the Sprite and Midget starting to sell more units combined than the Spitfire, although the margin was close. In fact, the rivalry between the trio had become more heated than ever, with the press more than content to fan the flames as seen in the following comments from *Autocar*:

> It would be difficult to find two more evenly matched cars. Their acceleration times differ by only a few tenths of a second and there is only 1 mph between their maximum speeds ... Both offer approximately the same accommodation and are aimed at the same market. Yet they differ enormously in character. The Midget is at its best when being hurled along a winding country road. Its beautifully light and precise gearchange encourages the driver to strive to get the best out of it and its low overall gearing merely adds to its nimbleness. The Spitfire, on the other hand, is a better proposition for long journeys on fast roads. Its higher gearing is an advantage under such conditions and its appeal can be further enhanced by specifying an overdrive.

In the minds of the motoring press and the public, it was hard to distinguish among them. 'But whichever one the buyer chooses,' wrote *Road & Track*, 'he is assured of many miles of motoring pleasure in the great sports car tradition. They're good cars, both of them. You can't go wrong.' As close as the two competitors were at the time, the gap between them would grow in later years, as safety requirements added increased weight, pollution controls strangled performance and the fortunes of their respective masters rose and fell following the formation of British Leyland in the spring of 1968.

A Sibling Rivalry

The landmark alliance marked the culmination of a period of rapid consolidation in the British automotive industry throughout the 1960s that had resulted in a number of mergers and acquisitions intended to create economies of scale that would enable the various parties to survive in the face of stiffening international competition and increasing regulatory demands. Admittedly, there were benefits to be gained from the union between BMC and Leyland, among them increased operating efficiencies, rationalization savings and access to capital on better terms, but these were returns that would require time to realize. In the short run, however, the massive conglomerate's various constituent entities found themselves in a pitched battle for the same customers and resource priority within the massive corporation.

Nowhere was this situation more acute than in the sports car market, where Austin-Healey, MG and Triumph all competed against one another with similar products, especially at the affordable end of the market. Where the competition among the bitter rivals had once been confined to the showroom floor, all three now had to fight for the same limited corporate resources at a time when the American government was implementing a host of new standards that threatened their very existence.

The first 'Federal' models arrived in 1969, marking the divergence of the Spitfire into two distinct species: one built for the North American market, with the other destined for the rest of the world. Customers in the United States received vehicles fitted with completely redesigned interiors, featuring fixed headrests, padded dashboards, revised switchgear and a matte finish for the walnut trim. The addition of primitive smog equipment forced the adoption of a lower 8.5:1 compression ratio and reduced the available power to 68 bhp at 5,500 rpm and 73 pound-feet of torque at 3,000 rpm. More troubling changes came the following year when the dual SU carburettors gave way to a single Zenith-Stromberg 150CD SE.

Curiously, the emasculated performance failed to resonate much at the time with customers and the press, as the Spitfire regained its position at the top of the sales charts in 1970. During a comparison test pitting the Mk III against the Austin-Healey Sprite, Datsun 1600 and Fiat 850 Spider, *Road & Track* discovered that the Triumph held up well against the competition: 'The straight-line acceleration of the Spitfire was the best of the four cars we tested and in top speed was only very slightly slower than the more powerful Datsun ... The ride of the Spitfire is also better than its live-axle competitors, especially on poorer road surfaces ... In summing up, we would fault the Spitfire on its swing-axle rear suspension, but praise it for its driving position, performance, comfortable ride, pleasant appearance and engine accessibility.'

The window glass remained unchanged from before, operating with the same handle and internal mechanism. The sun visor barely visible at the top of the image was an extra cost option.

This view displays the Spitfire's unparalleled engine compartment access and the generous luggage area in the boot. Adoption of the one-piece integrated bonnet and wing assembly allowed mechanics and do-it-yourself owners to tinker at will, though the lack of much protection beyond the inner wheel arches allowed the engine to accumulate significant dust and road grime.

The inner front wheel and double wishbones look like new in this immaculate restoration. Alford & Adler supplied the front suspension assembly, which utilised the same design as seen in the Herald but with a 1 inch wider track. The Spitfire boasted one of the most impressive turning circles ever recorded in a small sports car at 24 feet 2 inches. The disc brakes are the same Girling 9-inch units from the Herald 1200.

In order to comply with new American safety regulations, the front bumper was raised by 9 inches, resulting in an entirely new 'bone-in-the-mouth' appearance for the Spitfire Mk III. Impressively, the change was made without any significant alteration to the surrounding panels. The front indicators and sidelights were combined into a single unit positioned under the bumper, while the overriders gained rubber trim. Note the selective yellow headlights that identify this as an example that was originally sold in the French market.

As in the front, the rear quarter bumpers were also raised, forcing the elimination of the overriders, which otherwise would have obstructed the turn signal indicators and reversing lights. Late in the production run a new badge was added to the boot lid to replace the script seen here. At the same time the reversing lights and number plate light were combined into a single unit.

The Emperor's New Clothes

Despite such positive comments, there was no getting around the fact that the Spitfire was growing old. With the press tools starting to wear out, Triumph took the opportunity to freshen up the Spitfire's appearance to create a greater resemblance to the rest of the family, particularly the handsome Stag. While retaining the understructure and doors from the existing car, Michelotti performed his usual magic, penning tasteful changes that brought the styling into the 1970s. The exposed panel joints on the front fenders were eliminated and the entire rear end was redesigned to adopt the Kamm tail from the Stag and 2000 saloon. With subtle flared wheel arches, reduced brightwork, a flush rear deck and slimmer bumper blades that were integrated into the surrounding bodywork, the Mk IV represented a crisp and modern design that provided aesthetic consistency with the rest of the Triumph stable. Amazingly, only the sills and door skins remained from the old exterior panels, while a new, more angular hardtop, designed at Canley, complemented the redesign.

Introduced at the Turin Motor Show in October 1970, the Spitfire Mk IV was met with avidity for what it represented: British Leyland's continued commitment to one of its most important products. As one publication noted, it was 'a very much more civilized car, quieter and very pleasant drive', characteristics that continued to win new converts and please previous owners. Improving the driving experience was the new model's stock in trade. After almost unrelenting censure for the swing axle suspension, it was finally replaced with an ingenious 'swing-spring', which allowed the transverse leaf spring to pivot around a central pad, reducing roll stiffness to acceptable levels without compromising the vertical resistance necessary for daily driving.

In keeping with this theme, a fully synchromesh gearbox and an improved differential, based on components used in the GT6 and Vitesse, were installed, resulting in more comfortable operation at cruising speeds. Inside, the main instruments were moved from the centre of the dash to directly in front of the

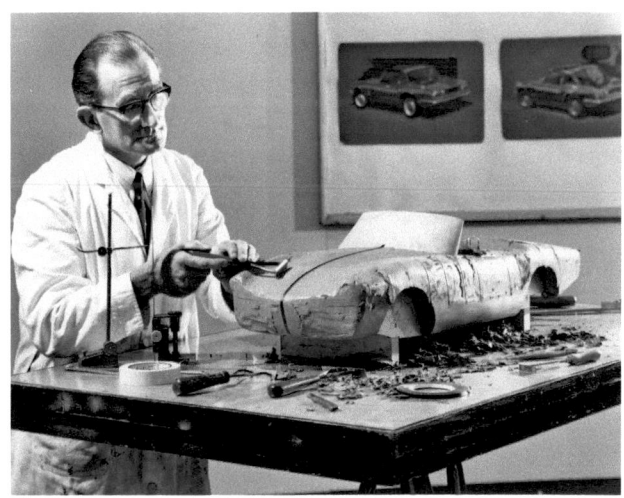

A clay model of the Spitfire Mk IV undergoes refinement in the Triumph styling studio. (Magic Car Pics)

driver, rocker switches replaced the previous controls and better seats appeared, while the optional overdrive could be operated from the shift lever rather than a stalk on the steering column.

Regrettably, these improvements added extra weight, causing the performance to backslide. Although the rated horsepower for rest of the world engines fell from 75 bhp to 63 bhp, the output actually remained the same, since the nominal loss reflected adoption of the DIN system, which calculated the available horsepower after subtracting the parasitic loss from ancillary equipment.

Triumph announced a new styling theme in late 1970, which resulted in the appearance of the Spitfire Mk IV. While retaining the basic platform, Michelotti freshened up the external panels to create a more modern vehicle that bore a strong familial resemblance to the rest of the Triumph model range. Although the plan to incorporate retractable headlights was abandoned to reduce production costs, the bonnet beading was eliminated for a crisper appearance and a Kamm tail added to increase the visual similarities between the 2000 and Stag.

The Spitfire Mk IV introduced a smoother bonnet and a fully integrated front bumper assembly. Note the rubber overriders and the prominent air dam that arrived in 1973. (Graham Robson Collection)

One of the most attractive elements of Michelotti's restyling effort was the slimmer front bumper assembly that was better integrated into the adjacent bodywork for a more organic appearance. Note the rubber overrider at the bottom of the frame, which was actually manufactured from black polycarbonate material. A new badge was attached to the bonnet, eliminating the need for the 'Triumph' lettering that had been used since the original Spitfire 4 in 1962.

In order to rationalise production with the crankshafts fitted to the larger 2-litre and 2.5-litre engines, the 1,296cc unit in the Spitfire Mk IV received larger main and big end bearings, which resulted in a minimal reduction in available horsepower due to increased internal friction. Because the new model weighed more than 50 lbs than before and had adopted a lower 3.89 final drive ratio, the time needed to accelerate from 0 to 60 mph increased to 16.2 seconds rather than the 14.5 seconds that it had taken in the Mk III. Note the new air filter box with dual intake trunks to supply cold air to the carburettors for improved volumetric efficiency.

With increasingly strict pollution standards in North America, Triumph was forced to install a milder camshaft in 1972, reducing the engine's output from 63 bhp at 6,000 rpm to 61 bhp at 5,500 rpm. Note the integrated windscreen frame, replacing the separate TR4-based assembly used previously.

The Spitfire Mk IV introduced an ignition ballast resistor to improve cold starting performance. On 1973 model vehicles a resistive wire built directly into the loom replaced this arrangement, as shown in this example.

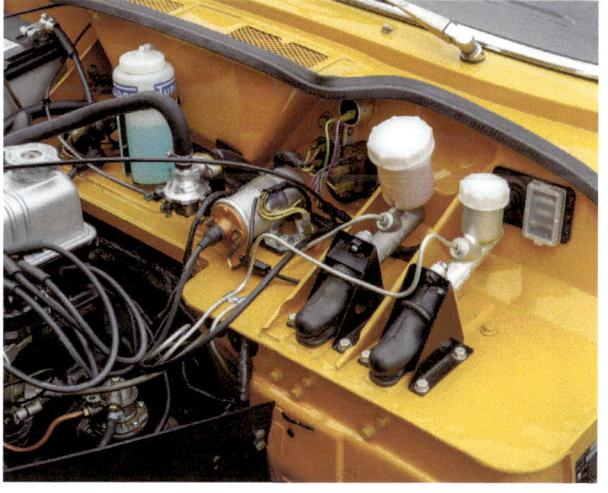

Spitfire Mk IV (1970–1974)

Engine:

Four cylinders in line. Cast-iron block and cylinder head.

Capacity:	1,296 cc
	1,493 cc (US: 1973–74)
Bore x Stroke:	73.7 mm x 76 mm
	73.7 mm x 87.5 mm (US: 1973–1974)
Valve Actuation:	Pushrod with overhead valves.
Compression Ratio:	9.0:1
	8.0:1 (US:1972)
Carburettors:	2 x SU HS2
	1 x Zenith-Stromberg 150 CDSE (US: 1972)
Output:	63 bhp (DIN) at 6,000 rpm
	58 bhp (DIN) (US: 1971)
	48 bhp (DIN) (US: 1972)
	57 bhp (DIN) at 5,000 rpm (US: 1973–74)
	69 pound-feet at 3,000 rpm
	74 pound-feet at 3,000 rpm (US: 1973–74)

Transmission:

Rear-wheel drive. Four-speed gearbox with synchromesh on all gears. Electric overdrive optional.

Suspension:

Front: Independent front suspension with coil springs and wishbones. Antiroll bar. Telescopic dampers.

Rear: Independent rear suspension with pivoting transverse spring. Telescopic dampers.

Steering:

Rack and pinion.

Brakes:

Front disc and rear drums.

Rolling Stock:

13-inch pressed steel or wire wheels. 145 x 13-inch tyres. 155 x 13-inch tyres from 1973.

Bodywork:

Separate chassis with steel panels.

Dimensions:

Length:	12 ft 5 in.
Wheelbase:	6 ft 11 in.
Front Track:	4 ft 1 in.
Rear Track:	4 ft 2 in. (From 1973)
Width:	4 ft 10½ in.
Height:	3 ft 11½ in.
Kerb Weight:	15.2 cwt

Performance:

Maximum Speed:	90 mph
0 to 60 mph:	16.2 sec.
Standing ¼ mile:	19.7 sec.

Production:

70,021

The Spitfire MK IV was available in both convertible and hardtop variants, although the hardtop could also be fitted to the convertible version. The frame assembly at the sides of the hood was covered in black plastic mouldings.

The boot received a durable floor mat and had hardboard panels fitted at either side. The jack was repositioned from the bracket attached to the inner wing structure into a pouch containing the vehicle's tool roll.

The wraparound rear bumper and flat rear deck lid created a strong resemblance to the Stag, although the larger vehicle adopted thinner taillight units that wrapped around into the extreme aft edge of the wings.

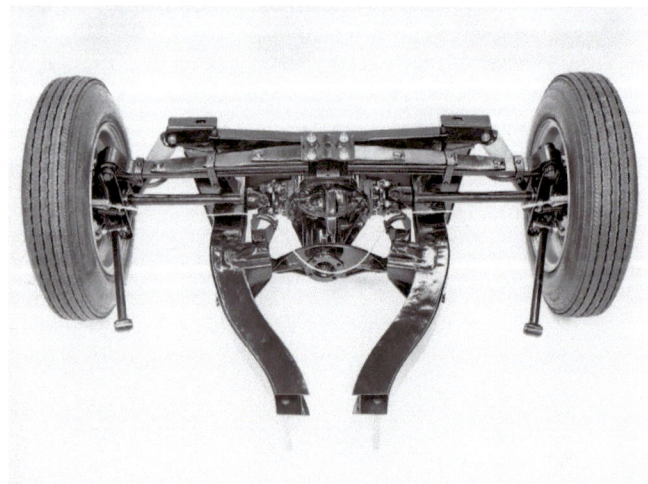

The simple but effective swing-spring independent rear suspension debuted in the Spitfire Mk IV to replace the original swing axle unit that had been inherited from the Herald. (Magic Car Pics)

In the United States, however, the revised horsepower classification could not alone account for the precipitous decline to 58 bhp, which was the result of stringent emissions requirements that were sucking the performance from all small-displacement sports cars. The situation grew worse in 1972, when even more restrictive smog equipment and an 8:1 compression ratio restricted the engine's output to only 48 bhp. With such scant power available, engineers reverted to the original 4.11:1 rear axle ratio to maintain acceleration at acceptable levels, which was more than could be said for the Midget. Meanwhile, the Sprite had vanished two years earlier, having fallen victim to British Leyland's decision to allow Donald Healey's consultancy agreement to expire, thus saving the royalties paid out for use of his name.

Damage Control

Although nothing could be done about the stricter emissions rules in America, Triumph was committed to keep the Spitfire competitive with the resources available on hand. A 'stroked' 1,493cc version of the Mk IV's 1,296cc engine had been used in the 1500 saloon since 1970, which provided Canley's engineers with an ideal solution to win back some of the lost performance in the North American market. While not a panacea, the larger engine represented a real improvement, producing 57 bhp at 5,000 rpm and 73 pound-feet of torque at 3,000 rpm in Federal trim.

The new engines were hastily installed in Spitfires sold in the American market during 1973, allowing the model to thrive at a time when rivals were disappearing at a rapid pace. All the effort at Canley did not go unnoticed, with *Road & Track* stating: 'All in all, we've got to give Triumph a lot of credit. Starting with what seemed like totally unsporting sedan components they have over the past decade transformed the Spitfire into a reasonably modern, handsomely styled, decent performing and good handling open roadster. Of the cars in its class the Spitfire is probably the best. That's not a statement we could have been made a few years ago, it says a lot for the evolution of the Spitfire.' Customers agreed; on 9 July 1973, the 200,000th Spitfire was driven off the production line at Canley, bound for a customer in California.

The rest of the world received the 1,493cc engine in December 1974, when a new model known as the Spitfire 1500 arrived. Freed from the burdens of American emissions equipment and retaining twin SU carburettors, the larger engine produced a respectable 71 bhp at 5,500 rpm and 82 pound-feet of torque at 3,000 rpm. The available power allowed the 1500 to reach 100 mph for the first time and resulted in better fuel economy, thanks to the use of a higher 3.63:1 final drive ratio. A 2-inch increase in the rear track improved dynamic stability and a larger diameter anti-roll bar compensated for the reduced roll-stiffness at the rear end to improve handling, providing the 1500 with the best road manners ever seen in a Spitfire. Unfortunately, these additions represented the model's final meaningful improvements, since British Leyland's attention and remaining cash were being directed to the TR7's troubled development.

In response to increasingly strict pollution measures in the North American market, Triumph provided the Spitfire with a larger 1,493cc engine to create the 1500 in 1973. The new powerplant allowed Canley to retain a performance advantage over its rival from Abingdon.

A bonnet decal in either black or silver identified the new model, which otherwise remained visually almost indistinguishable from its predecessor.

Despite the larger powerplant, American customers had to endure stagnant performance due to the replacement of the twin SU carburettor arrangement with a single unit from Zenith-Stromberg. With a reduced 7.5:1 compression ratio, output was restricted to 57 bhp at 5,000 rpm and 74 pound-feet of torque at 3,000 rpm. Examples destined for the rest of the world retained their SU carburettors and boasted 71 bhp at 5,500 rpm and 82 pound-feet of torque, allowing the 1500 to accelerate from 0 to 60 mph in 13.2 seconds and reach a 100 mph top speed.

Although very early examples were fitted with Spitfire Mk IV commission plates to use up the remaining stock, most received a new item containing the new model designation.

Apart from minor changes, early examples of the 1500 were fitted with the same interior as the Mk IV, but attractive cloth seats arrived in 1977 at the same time as steering column stalks sourced from the TR7. Note that the steering wheel is an aftermarket Moto Lita, rather than the thick-rimmed three-spoke item fitted as standard.

The 1500 boot featured carpeted surfaces for floor and both sides, although this example also displays carpeting on the forward panel. The vinyl cover for the spare wheel and tyre remained unaltered. Note the courtesy light that appeared to allow owners to find loose items in the boot at night without having to use a torch.

The chrome-plated luggage rack is an aftermarket item. Among the optional accessories available from the factory were the hardtop kit, overdrive, mud flaps, oil cooler, radio and speaker kit, competition brake pads and a laminated windscreen, which was made standard later in the production run.

Fitted with aftermarket alloy wheels and wider performance tyres, this 1975 1500 displays a purposeful stance, particularly due to the dual exhaust pipes. Note the British Leyland badge that is visible immediately forward of the bonnet latch. After October 1975, they were fitted on the right wing for vehicles supplied with right-hand drive, and the left wing for those with left-hand drive. The following year they were omitted completely.

Rest of the world examples retained the slim front bumper and modest overriders from the Mk IV until production ended in 1980. The angled lens on the combination light appeared from Commission Number 78,674 and resembled the unit that had been used on the Mk III.

As a bonus, however, Triumph fans had to smirk when MG suffered the ignominy of being forced to use the 1500 engine in the Midget 1500. A smaller steering wheel, additional courtesy lights, and a further reduction in compression ratio arrived in 1977, the latter another concession to worsening anti-pollution measures. As proof that a market remained for traditional sports car, sales actually improved between 1975 and 1978.

As the end of the road approached, Triumph was forced to install massive energy absorbent impact resistant front and rear bumpers in 1979 and 1980 North American models, mimicking the previous changes made to the MGB and Midget. Meanwhile, pollution laws in California had become so restrictive that Triumph were forced to withdraw the Spitfire from this important state in 1980, severely impacting North American sales. Although plans had been made to continue production until 1982, the situation in California, a rising exchange rate that was forcing prices to rise, and British Leyland's deteriorating financial condition sounded the Spitfire's death knell.

The final road test, published by *Road & Track*, read like an elegy: 'Few tears were shed over the MG Midget, BL's companion car to the Spitfire, when it was

Although less cumbersome than the grotesque appendages forced upon the MGB and Midget, Spitfires sold in North America from 1979 onward received massive energy absorbing bumpers both front and rear. The additional safety and smog equipment had a deleterious effect on the vehicle's overall weight, tipping the scales at 16.7 cwt (850 kg).

The final Spitfire rolls off the production line at Canley on 8 August 1980. A hand written placard reading 'There She Blows' is perched on the bonnet of this Home Market example. (Graham Robson Collection)

Spitfire 1500 (1975–1980)

Engine:

Four cylinders in line. Cast-iron block and cylinder head.

Capacity:	1,493 cc
Bore x Stroke:	73.7 mm x 87.5 mm
Valve Actuation:	Pushrod with overhead valves
Compression Ratio:	9.0:1
	7.5:1 (US)
Carburettors:	2 x SU HS2
	1 x Zenith-Stromberg 150 CDSE (US)
Output:	71 bhp (DIN) at 5,500 rpm
	57 bhp (DIN) at 5,000 rpm (US)
	82 pound-feet at 3,000 rpm
	74 pound-feet at 3,000 rpm (US)

Transmission:

Rear-wheel drive. Four-speed gearbox with synchromesh on all gears. Electric overdrive optional.

Suspension:

Front: Independent front suspension with coil springs and wishbones. Antiroll bar. Telescopic dampers.

Rear: Independent rear suspension with pivoting transverse spring. Telescopic dampers.

Steering:

Rack and pinion.

Brakes:

Front disc and rear drums.

Rolling Stock:

13-inch pressed steel or wire wheels. 155 x 13-inch tyres.

Bodywork:

Separate chassis with steel panels.

Dimensions:

Length:	12 ft 5 in.
	13 ft 1½ in. (Late US)
Wheelbase:	6 ft 11 in.
Front Track:	4 ft 1 in.
Rear Track:	4 ft 2 in. (From 1973)
Width:	4 ft 10½ in.
Height:	3 ft 11½ in.
Kerb Weight:	15.9 cwt

Performance:

Maximum Speed:	100 mph
	94 mph (US)
0 to 60 mph:	13.2 sec.
	15.4 (US)
Standing ¼ mile:	19.0 sec.
	20.2 sec. (US)

Production:

95,829

---

dropped in 1979. But the passing of the Spitfire is not so easy to accept. True enough, a much better small sports car could be built using the basic engineering of a modern front-drive sedan, and that is what British Leyland should do in replacing both the MGB and the Spitfire. But the beauty of the Spitfire – and this has characterized Triumph's other efforts, such as the nicely updated TR6 – is that it has kept reasonably current with skill and aesthetic understanding. In its own way, the Triumph Spitfire is still attractive after all these years.'

The last vehicle was completed at Canley in August 1980. Despite $500 rebates to move existing stock in the United States, the final examples remained unsold until 1981. Across eighteen years of production, Canley manufactured 314,332 Spitfires, selling 242,918 in North America. It was the best-selling British sports car in history but for the MGB, outselling the entire TR range almost two to one. The Bomb had grown into an unqualified success and became one of the most beloved sports cars in history. It would certainly be missed.

Chapter 4
Six Shooter

With the introduction of the Spitfire 4 and Vitesse Sports Six in 1962, following the TR4's successful debut the previous year, Triumph boasted Britain's most comprehensive range of affordable sporting cars. More importantly, customers, particularly those in North America, had welcomed the TR4 and Spitfire with fervour, helping to increase the company's market share considerably. At home, purchase tax reductions spurred domestic sales of mainstream saloons, which combined with strong export returns and firm Leyland stewardship to restore the oft-beleaguered enterprise to financial health. By 1963, the Triumph 2000 saloon, the replacement for the Standard Vanguard Six, was in final development for an October debut, and Project Ajax was underway to supersede the Herald with a modern successor boasting front-wheel drive and monocoque construction.

Shell Games

Amidst this bustle, Harry Webster was contemplating minor improvements to the Spitfire that would later bear fruit in the Mk II variant. He also had his own plan to develop an upmarket variant of the small sports car, specifically a grand touring version that would feature an enclosed bodyshell, rather than a removable hardtop. As usual, Webster asked Michelotti for his styling input, and received a series of promising sketches. The idea was first brought to the attention of the board of directors in August, and raised again at the final meeting of the year in December, but no decisions or further instructions were issued. Never one to wait for formal permission when the decision was obvious, Webster had already dispatched one of the original Spitfire developmental mules to Michelotti's studio in Turin for conversion into a prototype of the small grand touring concept.

Although a GT version of the Spitfire had been under consideration almost from the model's birth, none of the available engines were thought to provide the necessary performance, putting plans on hold until the 2-litre engine appeared on the scene. When the GT6 arrived in October 1966 it represented one of the most attractive, capable and affordable GT coupés on the market.

An early GT6 is seen during testing at MIRA with Fred Nicklin at the wheel. The prototype versions featured the Spitfire's split radiator grille and a broader bonnet bulge. (Graham Robson Collection)

That the task was completed by the end of the year speaks to the speed at which the Italian stylist worked. An attractive fastback roof with an opening tailgate was grafted to the existing bodywork, transforming the simple roadster into a proper coupé. Rather than retain the Spitfire's spartan interior, Michelotti envisioned a luxurious passenger cabin with full carpeting, comprehensive instrumentation set in a walnut trimmed dash and rally-style seats – all features befitting such an upmarket model.

When the prototype reached Canley, it was clear that Webster and Michelotti had worked a masterstroke, creating a model that would establish its own niche in the marketplace – the affordable grand touring car. On the road, however, the Spitfire GT proved less than compelling due to the extra weight from the steel roof and large glass backlight, negating the advantage of its aesthetic and practical appeal. By this time, however, management had warmed to the project and were eager to see what more could be done to further the design's development.

Fortunately, a solution was close at hand. The Vitesse Sports Six, also derived from the Herald, featured a small displacement 1,588cc six-cylinder unit that was thought capable of providing the necessary power and refinement. In early 1964, such an engine was installed in the Spitfire GT after moving the radiator forward and adding a prominent hood bulge with an open air intake to achieve the required clearance. Even with the additional brawn from the new engine, however, the resulting performance was still not much better than before, and less than needed to distance the car from its open sibling.

This same problem had also plagued the Vitesse, forcing the engineers to adopt the larger 1,998cc engine from the 2000 to address complaints from American customers that the car was too slow to justify its premium over the lesser Herald 1200, particularly as faster alternatives like the Ford Cortina Lotus had just entered the fray. In short order, the 1,588cc engine that had been installed in the Spitfire GT was replaced with a 1,998cc unit that provided the performance that had been desired all along.

The GT6 Mk I featured the same grille that later appeared on the Spitfire Mk III. The same lighting and front bumper were carried over from the contemporary Spitfire, although the overriders fitted were deeper than in the open car.

The original GT6 lacked louvres on the body behind the rear quarter windows. Note the pressed steel wheels and the single exhaust pipe that emitted a mellifluous exhaust note at speed.

The 1,998cc six-cylinder engine produced 95 bhp at 5,000 rpm and 117 pound-feet of torque at 3,000 rpm with twin Zenith-Stromberg 150 CD carburettors and a 9.5:1 compression ratio. The chrome valve cover was standard equipment while the PCV valve was a response to recent American measures to combat smog. Performance was similar to the TR4A with acceleration from 0 to 60 mph at 12 seconds and a top speed of 106 mph.

The length of the new powerplant forced the relocation of the radiator forward and lower when compared to its position in the Spitfire, but the engine's installation was otherwise achieved without modification of the forward bulkhead or chassis rails.

As management pondered what to do next, it learned that MG had begun work on its own grand touring car. This intelligence encouraged Triumph to order construction of two additional prototypes, each fitted with the larger engine and the uprated all-synchromesh gearbox that had just been developed for the works Spitfires, after the TR4 transmissions they had been using proved problematic during the 1964 racing season. Both cars adopted a new bonnet design, featuring a more streamlined power bulge and louvres to reduce heat in the engine compartment. Along the same lines, excessive cabin temperatures required the addition of opening quarter lights to increase interior air flow. The first prototype was constructed in the spring, and the second in the fall of 1965, giving rise to a new moniker to distance the model from its more proletarian sibling – the GT6.

For the rest of the year and well into 1966, final details were settled for production, including changes to the engine, driveline, suspension and brakes, all made to accommodate the higher performance available or rationalise production. An increase in the compression ratio to 9.5:1, combined with larger valves and a new intake manifold, raised power to 95 bhp at 5,000 rpm and 117 pound-feet of torque at 3,000 rpm. Production examples were fitted with a new final drive unit featuring larger differential gears, planet pinions, output shafts and bearings. Most vehicles fitted with overdrive received a 3.89:1 ratio, while those without had a 3.27 ratio.

Because of the six-cylinder powerplant's increased weight and the higher braking loads that were expected, larger front discs and Girling callipers were fitted, along with stiffer coil springs and an uprated antiroll bar. Most other front suspension components, including the vertical link, stub axle, wheel bearings and tie-rod lever, were sourced from the Vitesse, rather than the Spitfire. With larger 8-inch rear brakes, the rear hub back plates were increased in size accordingly, while later cars also had smaller rear wheel cylinders to provide better balance. Although better, albeit more expensive alternatives existed, the swing-axle independent rear suspension from the Spitfire carried over unaltered, except for a stiffer transverse leaf spring, softer damper settings and increased diameter drive shaft flanges.

By early summer, with the design finalised, the production department took over. Forward Radiator built the bodyshells using roof panels from Pressed Steel

GT6 Mk I (1966–1968)

Engine:

Six cylinders in line. Cast-iron block and cylinder head.

Capacity:	1,998cc
Bore x Stroke:	74.7 mm x 76 mm
Valve Actuation:	Pushrod with overhead valves
Compression Ratio:	9.5:1
Carburettors:	2 x Zenith-Stromberg 150 CD
Output:	95 bhp at 5,000 rpm
	117 pound-feet at 3,000 rpm

Transmission:

Rear-wheel drive. Four-speed gearbox with synchromesh on all gears. Electric overdrive optional.

Suspension:

Front: Independent front suspension with coil springs and wishbones. Antiroll bar. Telescopic dampers.

Rear: Independent rear suspension with transverse leaf spring and swing axles. Telescopic dampers.

Steering:

Rack and pinion.

Brakes:

Front disc and rear drums.

Rolling Stock:

13-inch pressed steel or wire wheels. 155 x 13-inch tyres.

Bodywork:

Separate chassis with steel panels.

Dimensions:

Length:	12 ft 1 in.
Wheelbase:	6 ft 11 in.
Front Track:	4 ft 1 in.
Rear Track:	4 ft 0 in.
Width:	4 ft 9 in.
Height:	3 ft 11 in.
Kerb Weight:	17.5 cwt

Performance:

Maximum Speed:	106 mph
0 to 60 mph:	12.0 sec.
Standing ¼ mile:	18.8 sec.

Production:

15,818

---

that were mated with the Spitfire's lower sheet metal and understructure to create the fastback profile. Although Harry Webster had thought that the GT6 would establish its own market niche, by the time that the first examples rolled out of Canley in July 1966, the MGB GT had already set the market – making it clear that the pair would have to compete for the same customers around the world.

Rapid Transit

The GT6 was unveiled on 19 October 1966 at the London Motor Show alongside the improved 2-litre Vitesse. With better performance than the more expensive and less refined MGB GT, the small Triumph had proven worth the wait. In a reversal of the plan used for the Spitfire's introduction, initial deliveries were earmarked for North America, while the UK and rest of the world did not receive customer deliveries until January 1967.

While its natural rival was the Abingdon-built coupé, the GT6 almost immediately received the sobriquet of the 'poor man's E-type'. Like the Jaguar, it offered an attractive silhouette, inline six-cylinder engine and a cosseting interior. Those similarities were not lost on the pundits. In the first American review of the little hardtop, *Road & Track* found much to admire: 'The GT6 is a smaller package that incorporates many of the same qualities that make the Jaguar E-type such an exhilarating car. It is smooth, it has good torque, low noise level and agility as well as stability in its handling. It's a great improvement over the Spitfire 4 from which it is descended. Not that the Spitfire 4 was bad, it's just that the GT6 is so much better. It has no parallel and it's worth the money.'

Admiration for the new model was just as favourable at home, but every road test also saw fit to mention the potential danger posed by the parsimonious decision to adopt the swing-axle suspension from the Spitfire, rather than the more effective but expensive system used in the 2000. In the relatively low-powered Spitfire, the simple suspension design offered good handling under most driving conditions. However, the high roll-centre had a tendency to produce rear end lift at high cornering speeds, allowing the rear wheels to tuck under, resulting in a severe transition to oversteer.

The Spitfire's light weight and quicker steering allowed an experienced driver to arrest this condition without drama, which could be entertaining in the right hands. The same situation in the faster and heavier GT6 could be downright hazardous, especially for the unsuspecting novice who released the throttle in mid-corner. American critics seemed more forgiving at first: 'One gets the feeling that the car has a degree of oversteer that can be enjoyed and utilized by a moderately skilled driver while never crossing up an unskilled one.' *Autocar* disagreed: 'We feel it is a pity that the limitations from the continued use of swing-axles should detract so much from what is basically such a good car and we urge Standard-Triumph to make improvements without delay.'

Despite this potential threat to life and limb, the GT6 arrived to great demand on both sides of the Atlantic, confirming that Harry Webster had the right idea from the start. Especially in the United States, which was considered the new model's primary market, there were customers waiting for a vehicle that combined the Spitfire's dexterity with the TR's performance.

Even with its host of attractive features, its small footprint limited the appeal, as Michael Cook remembered: 'Size was actually a marketing problem for the little GT because tall people did not fit in it, any more than they could sit up straight in a Spitfire with the factory hardtop. However, if you were under 6 feet and medium build, it fit snugly like a well-tailored suit.' Nonetheless, there were enough shorter customers around to keep the production line humming at a strong pace, with almost 16,000 examples sold of the original version, 80 per cent of which were sent to North America.

Seen in profile, the original GT6 is a strong contender for the most attractive sports car that Triumph built in the postwar era.

As befitting a proper GT, the GT6 featured a far more luxurious interior than was available in the Spitfire, with a full-width polished wood dash and a more logical instrument layout with the speedometer, rev counter and oil pressure gauge positioned in the driver's direct line of sight. Note the speaker located on the passenger side parcel shelf.

The headliner was supplied in white, making the somewhat cramped interior feel more spacious than was actually the case, especially for taller drivers who tended to feel claustrophobic due to the relatively low height of the upper windscreen frame. The opening rear quarter windows provided welcome ventilation in hot climates. Note the white plastic moulding that covers the hinges for the rear hatch and the courtesy light fitted in the assembly's centre.

With an opening rear hatch, the GT6 evoked natural comparisons to the Jaguar E-type. The carpeted floor featured a trimmed lip at the forward edge to prevent luggage or parcels from sliding forward into the seating area. The leather straps seen here were an extra cost option. The spare wheel and tyre are located in a special compartment under the floor of the luggage area.

The heated rear window and electric defroster were available at extra cost, although they appear to have been popular. Seen from the rear, the similarities between the GT6 and E-type seem less obvious, although the Triumph fastback boasts a similar attention to sporting detail that is altogether absent in the contemporary MGB GT.

Reducing the Risk

Despite the robust sales during the first two years of production, it was clear that something would have to be done to address the issue of the poor rear suspension design, which was considered the only serious chink in the armour. Introduced in July 1968 as the GT6+ in North America, and the GT6 Mk II in the rest of the world, the improved vehicle swept away the criticism that had plagued it before, particularly from the British motoring press.

Although engineers had already devised a simple remedy to tame the swing-axle suspension's disturbing tendencies (which would be used when the Spitfire IV was introduced in 1970), Harry Webster wanted a more sophisticated solution. His alternatives ranged from rather complex arrangements like the combined coil and spring strut layout that had been intended for the stillborn GT6R racecar to rudimentary camber compensators that had limited utility and were admittedly crude for such an upmarket vehicle.

In the end, Webster adopted a unique design that had been inspired by the Coopers that raced in Formula One during the late 1950s. The new layout retained

---

GT6 Mk II/GT6+ (1968–1970)

Engine:

Six cylinders in line. Cast-iron block and cylinder head.

Capacity:	1998 cc
Bore x Stroke:	74.7 mm x 76 mm
Valve Actuation:	Pushrod with overhead valves
Compression Ratio:	9.25:1
Carburettors:	2 x Zenith-Stromberg 150 CD
Output:	104 bhp at 5,300 rpm
	95 bhp at 4,700 rpm (GT6+)
	117 pound-feet at 3,000 rpm
	117 pound-feet at 3,400 rpm (GT6+)

Transmission:

Rear-wheel drive. Four-speed gearbox with synchromesh on all gears. Electric overdrive optional.

Suspension:

Front: Independent front suspension with coil springs and wishbones. Antiroll bar. Telescopic dampers.

Rear: Independent rear suspension with transverse leaf spring and swing axles. Telescopic dampers.

Steering:

Rack and pinion.

Brakes:

Front disc and rear drums.

Rolling Stock:

13-inch pressed steel or wire wheels. 155 x 13-inch tyres.

Bodywork:

Separate chassis with steel panels.

Dimensions:

Length:	12 ft 1 in.
Wheelbase:	6 ft 11 in.
Front Track:	4 ft 1 in.
Rear Track:	4 ft 1 in.
Width:	4 ft 9 in.
Height:	3 ft 11 in.
Kerb Weight:	17.8 cwt

Performance:

Maximum Speed:	107 mph (Mk II)
	106 mph (GT6+)
0 to 60 mph:	10.0 sec.
	11.0 sec. (GT6+)
Standing ¼ mile:	18.8 sec.
	18.0 sec. (GT6+)

Production:

12,066

A revised GT6 appeared in two distinct variants in October 1968: the GT6+ in North America and the GT6 Mk II for the rest of the world.

the transverse leaf spring, which also served as the top link, but added new lower wishbones that linked the hub and vertical link to the chassis. To accommodate variations in length and position while under load, engineers specified new driveshafts with Rotoflex rubber couplings to create an effective outer universal joint. The resulting geometry change from this double wishbone layout lowered the rear roll centre height considerably, from 12.8 inches to 6.3 inches, increased the rear track by 1 inch, and greatly reduced the possible range of rear camber changes. Tested by the competition department in 1967, this arrangement proved entirely successful in eliminating the tendency for the rear wheels to lift.

The Triumph marketing department described the GT6+/GT6 Mk II with the tagline 'More Sting in the Engine, More Cling in the Tail.' Webster's lower wishbone design provided the improved cling, while the TR5 supplied its sibling with the increased sting. When the TR5 was introduced at the 1967 London Motor Show, it featured a new full-width cylinder head that had been specifically designed for high-performance applications, featuring improved breathing and better volumetric efficiency. With this cylinder head, along with a new crankshaft, hotter camshaft and revised inlet manifold, power improved to 104 bhp for the rest of the world examples and 95 bhp for those sold in North America, allowing a top speed between 106 and 110 mph. Described in one road test headline as 'Better handling, quicker, more comfortable', it was certain that the GT6 had improved.

While nowhere near as troubling as the swing-axle suspension, high cabin temperatures, caused by poor air flow and radiated heat from the engine bay, had frustrated testers and customers since the model's initial introduction. A new ventilation system with 'eyeball' vents located in the dash panel and the footwells directed fresh air into the cabin, while additional louvres on the front wings and behind the rear quarter window helped to improve the flow. Other interior changes included matte finish on the dash trim, a new steering wheel, thinner seat cushions to increase the available headroom and an optional rear seat that could be used to carry very small children, helping to address the MGB GT's singular advantage over the GT6.

The practical side of the GT6 is apparent in this photograph, which reveals the unfettered access to the engine compartment and rear luggage area.

The engine used in the GT6+ and Mk II was actually a 2-litre version of the powerplant used in the TR5 and TR250. It featured a new full-width cylinder head that promoted better volumetric efficiency and allowed the installation of larger inlet and exhaust valves. Despite a slightly lower 9.25:1 compression ratio, the unit produced 104 bhp at 5,300 rpm thanks to a hotter camshaft, with available torque remaining the same as before at 117 pound-feet at 3,000 rpm.

A Lucas 15 ACR alternator was fitted as standard equipment with the Delco Remy D200 distributor carried over from the Mk I. The new powerplant also eliminated the exposed pushrod tubes on the cylinder head.

American safety legislation was beginning to have an effect on automotive interiors as the end of the 1960s approached. The gloss finish on the dash gave way to a matte finish while the exposed steering wheel spokes were sheathed in leather trim to protect against some unknown threat while the heater controls were recessed to prevent contact with them in a collision. Note the 'eyeball' vents in the dash and footwell, visible to the left of the dash bracket. The stalk to control the electric overdrive unit can be seen just below the speedometer.

All the instruments were flush mounted in the GT6+ and Mk II, while rocker switches proliferated in a concession to concerns over passenger safety in the event of a serious accident. The master light switch on the dash controlled the operation of the side and headlights; the stalk on the steering column was used to change the headlights from normal to high beams.

The seats in the GT6+ featured integrated headrests in the North American market and these appeared later in the Mk II for the rest of the world. As in the previous model, both seats could be tipped forward to access the rear compartment. Note the change to black for the moulding containing the hinges for the rear hatch.

Both the GT6+ and Mk II dispensed with the traditional Triumph badge and lettering in favour of a simple enamel bonnet badge. Although largely hidden from view, the aluminium grille is the same as in the Mk I.

In response to new safety regulations in the United States, both the GT6+ and Mk II featured a raised bumper, mirroring a similar change that appeared in the contemporary Spitfire Mk III.

Despite the significant improvements to the rear suspension and under the bonnet, the most visible differences between the original GT6 and its successors were the external changes made to match the styling of the Spitfire Mk III that arrived in 1967, featuring the bone-in-the-teeth front bumper and revised lighting details. To hold down costs, Rostyle wheel covers were made standard, with wire wheels made optional equipment.

Expectedly, response to the improved model was positive, with *Motor* finding: 'The new layout has banished the tendency to vicious oversteer that we had cause to criticise sharply in our last test and makes the GT6 a much safer and more predictable car.' Across the Atlantic, *Popular Imported Cars* praised the model as 'the only $3000 GT car with the smoothness of a high performance engine and independent suspension'.

Popular opinion seemed to concur, with *Car and Driver's* readers voting it the 'Best Sports/GT' model in its class, although the editors did not agree, calling the GT6+ 'a bleak, unfun, hard-to-drive sports car – which is to say, no sports car at all.' Despite these excoriating comments, the GT6 remained popular with customers due to its combination of performance and value. As *Road & Track* asked: 'Where else can you get a 6-cyl, 100+ mph coupe with a proper chassis, good finish and jazzy looks for $3,000? Nowhere we know of.'

The rear end of the new models featured raised rear quarter bumpers and new badges with white enamel backgrounds and chrome lettering. The reflector on the side of the rear wing was another concession made in compliance with new American safety standards.

Excessive cabin heat plagued the original GT6, leading to the installation of two 'eyeball' vents on the dash with additional vents added to provide fresh air to the footwells. To enhance air extraction from the cabin, these vents were added behind the rear quarter windows to increase ventilation.

There were few running changes made to the GT6+ and GT6 Mk II over their short production run. Almost all the revisions were introduced for the 1970 North American models, which saw structural enhancements to better meet Federal impact standards, revised pollution controls, reclining seats, better sound insulation and a new steering wheel. Externally, much of the previous chrome trim had given way to black replacements, complementing the windscreen frame, which was painted in matte black, a nod to changing tastes in the contemporary sports car market.

A Whole New World

Although the 1960s had been kind to the GT6, the following decade was less so, with declining sales, stricter American pollution standards and increased competition dimming its prospects. Introduced alongside the restyled Spitfire Mk IV at the 1970 Turin Auto Show in October, the GT6 Mk III benefitted from Michelotti's clever work in updating the tired design for a new decade. The fastback lines were rendered more attractive by the seamless front wings, slimmer bumpers and a deeper windscreen, while the Kamm tail at the rear allowed for better integration between the roof and rear deck.

The louvres were eliminated from the bonnet, which also featured a lower and wider power bulge, while the wings incorporated discreet flares at the wheel arches. New ventilated steel wheels, shared with the Spitfire Mk IV, were more

More important than the improved performance from the new engine under the bonnet, the GT6+ and Mk II greatly benefitted from the new rear suspension arrangement that retained the transverse leaf spring but added lower wishbones to the frame and wheel upright to create what was in effect an upper and lower wishbone package. Half-shafts with a flexible rubber coupling replaced the original axles to eliminate the dramatic camber fluctuations which had caused unsuspecting owners to flinch in fear when cornering with abandon, resulting in a much smoother vehicle with more genteel road manners.

modern and tasteful than the Rostyle wheel caps. Under the bonnet, the dual Zenith-Stromberg 150 CD SE carburettors were made adjustment-proof, and a new fan and ductwork were added to maintain commonality with the Spitfire. Inside, headroom benefitted from the deeper windscreen, with additional padding and flush-fitting instruments, controls and switchgear making the interior safer for the occupants.

Most marque authorities place the Mk III at the top of the GT6 pyramid, lavishing praise on its modern styling themes and luxurious interior, but several factors conspired to scuttle its future. With an energy crisis dampening enthusiasm for performance cars, there were fewer available customers in the market, and many of those were heading to Datsun's 240Z. Introduced in 1970, the Japanese coupé occupied the same price class as both the GT6 and MGB GT, but boasted more performance and better construction quality than either could provide. With more power available from its larger engine, the 240Z was also better equipped to deal with the onslaught of pollution standards that were strangling the life out of British sports cars.

Pollution standards were causing havoc throughout the industry, but the effects were often worse for British Leyland, which lacked the funds to arrive at more effective solutions. In 1972, American GT6s suffered from more stringent smog controls, reducing output from 90 bhp to 79 bhp, although the rest of the world examples avoided the same fate. Mike Cook recalls the impact that the rules had

The GT6 tracked the changes introduced for the contemporary Spitfire throughout its life. This Mk III variant features a smoother bonnet with a reprofiled bulge, rubber overriders, and a windscreen that is 2 inches deeper than before. (Graham Robson Collection)

The GT6 Mk III that arrived in 1970 succeeded both the GT6+ and Mk II around the world and incorporated Triumph's new corporate styling theme with a smoother bonnet and crisper rear end treatment. Mirroring the styling changes that appeared in the Spitfire Mk IV, the final iteration of the GT6 formula appeared even more modern and contemporary than ever before.

on performance: 'This was the era when engine design had not caught up to Federal regulations and all manufacturers were meeting emissions standards by any means that allowed the cars to be reasonably drivable. Vacuum controlled distributor advance and retard meant that Triumph engines did not always return to idle speed during shifts, making smooth shifting difficult. The retarded timing caused very sluggish response when accelerating from rest. Until fuel injection became common and computerized engine management was developed, the old-style carburetted cars with emission controls and standard distributors with points could not match the performance of Triumphs from the early 1960s.'

Whether the cause was a declining market, increased competition or diminished performance, GT6 sales dropped almost 10 per cent in 1972. Distressingly, demand fell further the following year. To reduce production costs, the final 4,218 Mk IIIs saw the double wishbone Rotoflex suspension abandoned in favour of the less expensive 'swing-spring' layout used in the Spitfire. Inside, brushed cloth inserts were used on the seats, and new instruments, tinted glass and a smaller steering wheel were added. An improved alternator, the Lucas

16ACR, was installed, as were upgraded brakes, with servo-assistance made a standard feature.

As British Leyland struggled to adapt to changing market conditions, and beset by continued financial problems, it made little sense to continue producing two cars that competed directly head-to-head. With steadily declining sales, and even more stringent American pollution and safety regulations on the horizon, it made sense to eliminate the GT6 altogether. Despite the impending death sentence, the GT6 remained a formidable competitor. During a massive nine-car on-track comparison test conducted by *Road & Track* in 1973, it was not without surprise that the GT6 held its own against competitors from Fiat, MG, Opel, Porsche and VW: 'Does everything well. Plenty of power, gearing that lets the power be used in these conditions and good brakes. The car's natural understeer brings it around the fast sections under control, and the power lets the driver fling the car around in the tight turns.'

With declining sales for the GT6 Mk II, Triumph was forced to provide the model with the same styling revisions made across the rest of the corporate range in an attempt to stem the loss of consumer interest. Unfortunately, increasingly stringent American anti-pollution regulations reduced the available performance significantly as time passed, further dampening demand in Triumph's most important export market.

The Mk III debuted with the same engine used in the previous version, but a change in the way that the output was measured resulted in an apparent decline in horsepower to 98 bhp at 5,300 rpm. In the United States, new emissions requirements steadily eroded the available power, which fell to 90 bhp at 4,700 rpm in 1971 and 79 bhp at 4,900 rpm in 1972 and 1973, making the Federal version of the GT6 not much faster than a Spitfire in Home Market trim. Note that the alternator fan has been fitted with a protective shield due to its proximity to the bonnet stay.

In order to meet recently introduced anti-smog measures, twin tamper-proof Zenith-Stromberg 150 CDSE carburettors were fitted. Note the use of a cable-mounted accelerator linkage, the first time that such a system appeared on a GT6. Barely visible is the seven-bladed pale yellow plastic cooling fan behind the dual trunks for the air filter assembly.

The central bonnet bulge was made lower and wider, while the cooling louvres were completely removed. The chin spoiler arrived in 1973 at the same time that it appeared on the Spitfire Mk IV. Note that this particular example lacks a bonnet badge.

The GT6 utilised the same narrow front bumper and light assemblies as seen on the contemporary Spitfire Mk IV. Note the new bonnet badge that replaced the white enamel item used in the GT6+ and Mk II.

The rear appearance of the Mk III was similar to the Spitfire Mk IV, though the trim surrounding the rear panel was a continuous strip since it did not have to accommodate an opening boot lid.

The cabin vent was increased in length and the cover was painted in body colour. Note that the beading on the rear wing is black rather than chrome as in previous examples.

The interior of the Mk III featured few obvious changes beyond the fact that the ignition key was relocated to a spot beneath the steering column, where it was incorporated with an integral steering lock. Note the increased width of the clutch and brake pedals and the new steering wheel design shared with the TR6 and Spitfire Mk IV.

Occupants in the GT6 Mk III benefitted from a 2-inch deeper windscreen assembly, which enhanced the interior's spaciousness and allowed in more ambient light. The late style seats seen in this 1972 Federal model provided greater comfort than the older units and were often trimmed with corduroy cloth. The medallion on the dash honours the SCCA National Championships that the GT6 recorded in 1969 and 1970.

Recessed pull-style door handles with chrome escutcheons replaced the push-button units used in previous examples.

GT6 Mk III (1970–1973)

Engine:

Six cylinders in line. Cast-iron block and cylinder head.

Capacity:	1,998cc
Bore x Stroke:	74.7 mm x 76 mm
Valve Actuation:	Pushrod with overhead valves
Compression Ratio:	9.25:1
	8.0:1 (US: 1972–73)
Carburettors:	2 x Zenith-Stromberg 150 CD
Output:	104 bhp at 5,300 rpm
	90 bhp (US: 1971)
	79 bhp (US: 1972–73)
	117 pound-feet at 3,000 rpm
	116 pound-feet at 3,400 rpm (US:1971)
	97 pound-feet at 2,900 rpm (US: 1972–73)

Transmission:

Rear-wheel drive. Four-speed gearbox with synchromesh on all gears. Electric overdrive optional.

Suspension:

Front: Independent front suspension with coil springs and wishbones. Antiroll bar. Telescopic dampers.

Rear: Independent rear suspension with pivoting transverse leaf spring from February 1973. Telescopic dampers.

Steering:

Rack and pinion.

Brakes:

Front disc and rear drums.

Rolling Stock:

13-inch pressed steel or wire wheels. 155 x 13-inch tyres.

Bodywork:

Separate chassis with steel panels.

Dimensions:

Length:	12 ft 5 in.
Wheelbase:	6 ft 11 in.
Front Track:	4 ft 1 in.
Rear Track:	4 ft 1 in.
	4 ft 2 in. (From February 1973)
Width:	4 ft 9 in.
Height:	3 ft 11 in.
Kerb Weight:	17.8 cwt

Performance:

Maximum Speed:	107 mph
	104 mph (US)
0 to 60 mph:	10.0 sec.
	12.6 sec. (US)
Standing ¼ mile:	18.8 sec.
	19.6 sec.

Production:

13,042

When the end arrived, it approached at a deliberate pace. Over three years of production, 13,042 Mk IIIs were manufactured in total, but when the final GT6 rolled out of Canley in November 1973, only three others had been built that same month. Despite the painful end, there is little doubt that the GT6 had been a successful entrant in a market segment that was almost unknown at the time of its creation, with 40,926 built from 1966 to 1973, and approximately 24,581 of those sold in the United States. The GT6 was the first mass-produced British sports car to meet its demise during the troubled decade – it would not be the last.

Chapter 5
In Competition

With Kenneth Richardson's steady hand at the helm, Triumph's competition programme experienced a fair amount of success on the international scene in both rally and racing events. Despite an improbable team prize with the TRS at the 24 Hours of Le Mans in 1961, which represented one of the era's best results, Leyland management shuttered the entire operation almost immediately afterward to reduce expenses at a time when cash was in limited supply.

Never one to accept such a poorly reasoned decision without a fight, Harry Webster managed to relaunch the works team later that year with Graham Robson, a recently hired engineer who had prior rally experience with Sunbeam, in charge as the Competitions Secretary. With a renewed emphasis on reliability, the TR4 proved a worthy adversary, but by 1963 it was clear that it was reaching the end of its competitive life, leading to the decision that the Spitfire would be used for tarmac rallies and circuit racing, and the 2000 saloon reserved for rally events conducted over rougher surfaces, where its more rugged construction and better ground clearance conferred a clear advantage.

Return to France
Webster also mandated a return to the 24 Hours of Le Mans in 1964 after a three-year hiatus, assigning John Lloyd the task of preparing a team of Spitfires that would run as prototypes in the 1.3-litre class, freeing them from the restrictions required of production machinery. In order to maximise the top speed down the Mulsanne Straight, the fastback profile later used for the GT6 was adopted using aluminium shells and fibreglass roofs, with Perspex used for the side windows and backlight to reduce weight. An impressive increase in available power resulted from a new cylinder head with eight ports, revised camshaft profiles, and tuned inlet and exhaust manifolds. With an increased compression ratio of 11.75:1, twin Weber carburettors and a less restrictive exhaust, output rose to 98 bhp at 6,750 rpm, allowing the vehicles to reach 134 mph. For better reliability, Lloyd also specified the robust TR4 gearbox, replacing what had been perceived as a weak link in the standard kit.

In contrast to the highly modified drivetrain, minimal changes were made to the suspension, save for adjustable dampers at all four corners, and modifications made to increase the overall stiffness and improve the geometry for the transverse leaf spring in the rear. While these revisions reduced the body roll considerably, they also exacerbated the tendency for abrupt camber changes in the rear wheels, leading to some tense moments in the corners. With greater brake power required, the diameter of the front rotors was increased to 9.5 inches, while larger drums were used in the rear.

The works team in the pits at the 24 Hours of Le Mans in 1964. ADU 1B was driven by Americans Mike Rothschild and Bob Tullius, ADU 2B by future Formula One presenter David Hobbs and Rob Slotemaker, and ADU 3B by Frenchmen Jean-Louis Marnat and Jean-François Piot. ADU 2B was the only example to complete the race, finishing third in class and twenty-first overall, behind a pair of Alpine A110s. (Graham Robson Collection)

While four cars were ultimately prepared, only three contested the actual event, each assigned an international driving crew. Americans Mike Rothschild and Bob Tullius were assigned to drive in ADU 1B, Britons David Hobbs and Rob Slotemaker in ADU 2B, while Frenchmen Jean-Louis Marnat and Jean-Francois Piot helmed ADU 3B. With the Spitfire's rally debut set for the following week at the Alpine Rally, Lloyd and Lyndon Mills oversaw the operation in France, while Robson prepared his rally team for the arduous trek across the Continent.

Although testing at the Circuit de la Sarthe in April had shown the worthiness of the aerodynamic modifications, which were improved in time for the actual event with the addition of faired-in headlamps, there was little expectation that teething problems with the untried drivetrain could be entirely avoided. Despite engine speeds of 7,000 rpm on the fastest sections, the running gear proved perfectly reliable, though two of the three cars retired prematurely due to shunts on the track. Salvaging matters for Triumph, however, Hobbs and Slotemaker had a rather uneventful run, finishing twenty-first overall for third in class honours, ahead of the Donald Healey Motor Company's Sprite and another pair of French competitors.

At the Alpine Rally, Triumph experienced a similar result, with only a solitary representative running at the finish, although Rauno Aaltonen took home a Coupes des Alpes and Terry Hunter missed out on another by the smallest of margins. With aerodynamic advantage less important than durability in such events, the rally vehicles used steel shells with external aluminium panels and standard hardtops, each fitted with the gearbox from the Vitesse and aluminium cylinder heads, in contrast to the cast-iron heads used in the racing cars.

During the Tour de France in September, fastback roofs were added, along with a prototype all-synchromesh gearbox intended for eventual use in the GT6. A gruelling event that combined several circuit races along with the traditional rally stages, the Alpine exacted a fierce toll on the competitors, forcing the retirement of two machines after the first day, leaving the other pair to carry the torch for the remaining nine days. An engine casualty in the French Alps claimed the unfortunate Thuner, which left Slotemaker to claim a class victory while finishing tenth overall in the GT category, soundly defeating Alpine-Renault on its own turf. Success continued during the remainder of the Spitfire's maiden year competition, with Thuner taking another class victory in the Paris 1,000 km race and Hunter finishing first in the GT category at the Geneva Rally, which also saw Triumph take home the team prize as an added bonus.

The works rally team pictured at Canley prior to the 1964 Tour de France. The trio were originally fitted with standard hardtops but were converted to fastback trim following their appearance at the French Alpine Rally earlier in the year, where ADU 7B finished third in class. (Graham Robson Collection)

ADU 7B and ADU 5B on the grid at the 1964 Tour de France, where Standard-Triumph competed with the entire works team. ADU 5B was assigned to Jean-Jacques Thuner and John Gretener, ADU 6B to Roy Fidler and Bill Bradley, and ADU 7B to Rob Slotemaker and Terry Hunter. Despite stiff competition from teammates Thuner and Gretener and the works Alpine Renaults, Slotemaker and Hunter managed to win their class, finishing fifth overall in the GT category and tenth overall on scratch – finishing behind four Ferrari GTOs, four Porsche 904s and an Alfa Romeo. (Graham Robson Collection)

Flush with confidence, Triumph expected even better results in 1965, but started the year off with a second in class at Monte Carlo behind a strong run from Slotemaker, who helmed the only Spitfire still running at the finish. With Robson's departure for a career in motoring journalism, responsibility for the team's management then passed to Ray Henderson and Gordon Birtwhistle.

In North America, R. W. 'Kas' Kastner managed Triumph's North American competition effort, while also lending parts and technical support to various privateers. Blessed with a true gift for extracting maximum performance from his equipment, Kastner had won an SCCA national championship in a TR3A, leading to a management position with Cal Sales in Los Angeles, while continuing his successful career as an amateur racer. In 1960, Standard-Triumph assumed control of the Cal Sales operation, forcing Kastner out of the cockpit and into control of the factory operation after a solid showing at the 1963 12 Hours of Sebring.

NOTABLE INTERNATIONAL COMPETITION RESULTS

YEAR	EVENT	DRIVER(S)	RESULT
1964	Welsh Rally	Roy Fidler	Second overall
1964	French Alpine Rally	Terry Hunter	Third in class
1964	Tour de France	Rob Slotemaker	First in class
1964	Geneva Rally	Terry Hunter	Second overall, First in GT Category
1964	Geneva Rally	Jean-Jacques Thuner	Fifth overall
1964	Paris 1,000 km	Jean-François Piot/Jean-Louis Marnat	First in class
1964	24 Hours of Le Mans	David Hobbs/Rob Slotemaker	21st overall, third in class
1965	Monte Carlo Rally	Rob Slotemaker	Second in class
1965	Monte Carlo Rally	Simo Lampinen	Third in class
1965	12 Hours of Sebring	Ed Barker/Diane Feuerhelm	29th overall, second in class
1965	12 Hours of Sebring	Bob Tullius/Charlie Gates	30th overall, third in class
1965	Geneva Rally	Jean-Jacques Thuner	First in class
1965	Geneva Rally	Simo Lampinen	Second in class
1965	French Alpine Rally	Simo Lampinen	First in Prototype Category
1965	French Alpine Rally	Jean-Jacques Thuner	Second in Prototype Category
1965	24 Hours of Le Mans	Jean-Jacques Thuner/Simo Lampinen	13th overall, first in class
1965	24 Hours of Le Mans	Claude Dubois/Jean-François Piot	14th overall, second in class
1967	12 Hours of Sebring	Richard Kondracki/Ray Pickering	32nd overall, second in class

In sharp contrast to Richardson, who ran his competition cars in almost standard tune, Kastner believed in pushing machinery to the absolute limit, resulting in much faster vehicles than those seen across the pond. In 1965, Kastner returned to Florida for the Grand Prix of Endurance at Sebring, running a team of Spitfires in Le Mans trim, complete with their aluminium bodyshells and gearboxes from the GT6. Despite horrendous weather, Spitfires finished second and third in class behind a works Midget in aerodynamic trim, marking Abingdon's sole victory over Canley in the small car class during international competition.

The works team seen at the 1965 12 Hours of Sebring, which was run in a torrential downpour despite temperatures in excess of 34 degrees. ADU 1B was driven by Peter Bolton and Mike Rothschild, ADU 2B by Bob Tullius and Charlie Gates, and ADU 4B by Ed Barker and Diane Feuerhelm. Barker and Feuerhelm finished twenty-ninth overall and second in class with Tullius and Gates one spot back at thirtieth overall and third in class. (Graham Robson Collection)

A few months later at Le Mans, the Spitfires competed as homologated GT cars, rather than in the prototype class, boasting considerable weight savings over the previous year thanks to a smaller gearbox and rear brake drums, as well as a chassis frame constructed from thinner steel and an aluminium cylinder head. With four cars competing instead of the usual three, Thuner and Simo Lampinen were drafted from the rally team to flush out the ranks. Benefitting from a full year's experience, Triumph captured first and second in class, representing the best finish in the Spitfire's brief international racing career. The rally drivers Thuner and Lampinen validated their selection, finishing thirteenth overall, finishing one spot ahead of their teammates Claude Dubois and Jean-François Piot. The fact that the Spitfires were the final two finishers tempered satisfaction for the victory to some extent, as all the remaining thirty-seven competitors fell out along the way, but the result paid clear dividends from a marketing perspective.

With pending changes to the FIA's Appendix J regulations threatening to render the Spitfire uncompetitive, however, the 1965 outing at the Circuit de la Sarthe marked the Spitfire's final appearance in international racing competition, although Bill Bradley, running as a privateer, albeit benefitting from factory support, managed to carry the torch forward into the new year, winning his class fourteen times in eighteen events.

ADU 3B returned to Le Mans in 1965, where it was assigned to Jean-François Piot and Belgian Claude Dubois. The pair finished an impressive second in class behind their teammates Jean-Jacques Thuner and Simo Lampinen. (Magic Car Pics)

Not long before the race, Triumph was allowed to field a fourth entry, which was assigned to rally drivers Jean-Jacques Thuner and Simo Lampinen. Wearing registration number ADU 4B, the Spitfire finished thirteenth overall and won the GT 1.15 displacement class. (Graham Robson Collection)

On the other side of the operation, the rally team continued its successful run through to the end of 1965, securing a first and second in class at the Geneva Rally and an overall win in the prototype category for Thuner and Lampinen in the French Alpine Rally. The pair benefitted immensely from Harry Webster's decision to develop a 1,296cc engine, which produced an impressive 117 bhp at 7,000 rpm and 97 foot-pounds of torque at 5,500 rpm, making for a much faster mount than ever before.

Only recently returned from France, Triumph's engineers then set out to build a bespoke racer for Standard-Triumph's Hong Kong distributor, Walter Sulke, who wanted a car to race at the Grand Prix of Macau, which was the only event on the international calendar that allowed true amateurs to compete alongside the ranks of professionals that comprised a typical grid.

Built from existing parts in stock, the highly modified creation resembled a scaled-down sports racer, built around an aluminium shell with a fibreglass rear deck. With a streamlined headrest behind the driver and a rigid tonneau over the passenger compartment, it represented a considerable visual departure from the Le Mans competitors, particularly due to the wider tires and cut-down windscreen.

Simo Lampinen during the 1965 Alpine Rally, where he piloted AVC 654B to a win in the Prototype category despite the presence of the vaunted Porsche 904 in the same group. Earlier that year, the driver and vehicle pairing finished third in class at the Monte Carlo Rally and second in class at the Geneva Rally, with the only failure to finish recorded at the Tulip Rally. (Magic Car Pics)

The revised coachwork was extensively tested in the wind tunnel, allowing the streamlined vehicle to reach speeds approaching 130 mph. (Magic Car Pics)

Walter Sulke, Standard-Triumph's distributor in Hong Kong, commissioned this special lightweight racer for the Macau Grand Prix. It was built on an all-aluminium tub with a rigid tonneau cover over the passenger compartment, a fairing behind the driver's seat, and a fibreglass rear deck. It finished third overall in the main race before heading to California where Kas Kastner campaigned it with moderate success. (Magic Car Pics)

The highly tuned powerplant, essentially similar to the Le Mans powerplant, produced 109 bhp at 7,200 rpm, allowing a 130 mph top speed due to the aerodynamic bodywork. After a third place finish at Macau, the car returned home before heading to California, where Kastner installed a 2-litre from the GT6, campaigning it in the SCCA's D-Modified class.

Harry Webster entertained similar thoughts in an attempt to fend off the Spitfire's obsolescence, installing the 2000's 2-litre powerplant combined with triple Weber carburettors and the cylinder head later used in the TR5 and GT6 into a Le Mans chassis, though adoption of Lucas petrol injection was contemplated for the future, in order to create what was dubbed internally as the GT6R. Unfortunately, the proposal was abandoned after the competition programme was pared down in early 1966, leaving the sole example little more than a primitive mule, although the lessons learned during its construction would aid later projects.

America proved the most fertile ground for the Spitfire's success, typically while outfitted in Group 44 Inc.'s iconic green and white livery. Based out of

Pictured with his son Jerry, Ed Barker was one of the most accomplished privateers in the United States. Barker notched up thirty overall victories in a Spitfire and an additional eleven class wins, among them a 1964 SCCA G Production National Championship. Jerry Barker accomplished the same feat in 1980, taking the SCCA F Production National Championship. (Plain English Archive)

Fairfax, Virginia, Tullius had formed the team after securing a D Production national championship and a victory in the American Road Race of Champions with a TR4, holding his entire staff to a professional standard despite their nominal amateur status. A master promoter, talented driver, and an intense competitor, Tullius expected to dominate the competition and did so on a regular basis. With drivers such as Tony Adamowicz, Brian Furstenau and John Kelly, Group 44's Spitfires were a seemingly unstoppable force, but others also had their fair share of success. Including Group 44's results in the total, Spitfires amassed an unbelievable number of victories, including an unprecedented twenty-nine SCCA National Championships in various classes, continuing to claim them well into the twenty-first century, more than thirty years after the last Spitfire rolled off the production line.

Although the GT6 never competed in factory colours at home, both Kastner's factory-supported drivers and Group 44 campaigned the model to fair success, running alongside the TR4A and Spitfire at events across the country. With little experience, however, in tuning the six-cylinder engine for maximum performance and reliability, particularly since petrol injection was not permitted

Triumph achieved exceptional value from its association with Group 44 in the United States, putting the distinctive green and white-liveried racecars on prominent display at the New York Auto Show and other events held across the country. (Plain English Archive)

John Kelly behind the wheel of the Group 44 Spitfire in 1971. The previous year, Kelly had won the 1970 SCCA F Production National Championship, finishing ahead of Jerry Barker and Ken Slagle, securing all three spots on the podium for the Spitfire. (Bob Tullius)

under the SCCA's rules, making it difficult to keep the cars running at the front of the pack. With little to no help from the factory, Kastner and Tullius had to work out the problems for themselves, sharing information whenever possible, despite their status as nominal competitors. The GT6's rear suspension proved especially problematic, combining the worst traits of the Spitfire's unit with far more power, making it a real hazard to circulate around the track free from drama. Eventually, most of the problems were resolved satisfactorily, allowing Mike Downs and Don Devendorf to capture consecutive SCCA National Championships in 1969 and 1970.

As would the Spitfire, the GT6 continued to run in SCCA competition with privateer drivers well after Kastner and Group 44 had moved on to more modern British Leyland equipment, though it never experienced the continued success that has made the Spitfire a legend in North American racing. In the modern era, several vintage racers campaign the model on both sides of the Atlantic, further burnishing its competition laurels and adding to the allure of the Triumph marque, proving the inherent excellence of the original platform in both four- and six-cylinder versions.

Brian Furstenau on the track in a Group 44 GT6 during the 1972 SCCA racing season. The lanky driver had secured an SCCA F Production National Championship in a Spitfire four years earlier and repeated the feat in 1973. (Bob Tullius)

\\	SCCA NATIONAL CHAMPIONSHIPS		
YEAR	DRIVER	MODEL	CLASS
1964	Ed Barker	Spitfire	GP
1968	Don Devendorf	Spitfire	GP
1968	Brian Furstenau	Spitfire	FP
1969	Mike Downs	GT6	EP
1969	Lee Mueller	Spitfire	FP
1970	Don Devendorf	GT6	EP
1970	John Kelly	Spitfire	FP
1971	Marshall Meyer	Spitfire	GP
1972	Rick Cline	Spitfire	GP
1973	Rick Cline	Spitfire	GP
1973	Brian Furstenau	Spitfire	EP
1973	John Kelly	Spitfire	FP
1974	Rick Cline	Spitfire	FP
1975	Ken Slagle	Spitfire	FP
1975	Jerry Barker	Spitfire	GP
1977	Tom Collier	Spitfire	FP

1978	Jack May	Spitfire	FP
1979	Steve Johnson	Spitfire	FP
1980	Jerry Barker	Spitfire	FP
1992	Steve Sargis	Spitfire	FP
1993	Steve Sargis	Spitfire	GP
1996	Dean C. Johnson	Spitfire	GP
2002	Steve Sargis	Spitfire	FP
2004	Tom Feller	Spitfire	HP
2005	Tom Feller	Spitfire	HP
2006	Tom Feller	Spitfire	HP
2007	Tom Feller	Spitfire	HP
2010	Steve Sargis	Spitfire	HP
2011	Steve Sargis	Spitfire	FP
2012	Steve Sargis	Spitfire	FP

Mike Downs won an SCCA E Production National Championship with this GT6 in 1969. Note the magnesium alloy wheels and wide Goodyear racing tyres. (Bob Tullius)

British Leyland supplied special dash badges to Spitfires sold in the North American market, showing the model's victories in SCCA competition. (Cape Coventry Racing)

Bibliography

Carver, Mike, and Nick Seale and Anne Youngson, *British Leyland Motor Corporation: 1968–2005 The Story from Inside*. (Stroud: The History Press, 2015)

Clarke, R. M. (Compiler), *Triumph Spitfire: 1962–1980*. (Surrey: Brooklands Books)

Clarke, R. M. (Compiler), *Triumph Spitfire Gold Portfolio: 1962–1980*. (Surrey: Brooklands Books)

Cook, Michael, *Triumph Cars in America*. (St Paul: Motorbooks International, 2001)

Dredge, Richard, *Triumph Spitfire and GT6: The Complete Story*. (Wiltshire: Crowood, 2014)

Harvey, Chris, 'Triumph Before Tragedy' Automobile Quarterly 28 (1990) 10-29

Kastner, Kas, *Kas Kastner's Historical & Technical Guide for Triumph Cars*. (Vista: R. W. Kastner, 2008)

Kastner, Kas, *Kas Kastner's Triumphs: Race Cars, Street Cars and Special Cars*. (Vista: R. W. Kastner, 2010)

Krause, G. William, *Triumph Sports Cars*. (St. Paul: Motorbooks International, 1998)

Krause, G. William, *Triumph Sports and Racing Cars*. (Forest Lake: Car Tech, 2017)

Newton, Richard, *Illustrated Triumph Buyer's Guide*. (Osceola: Motorbooks International, 1994)

Nikas, John, *Rule Britannia: When British Sports Cars Saved a Nation*. (Philadelphia: Coachbuilt Press, 2017)

Nye, Doug, *British Cars of the Sixties*. (Stillwater: Parker House, 2008)

Piggott, Bill, *Triumph: The Sporting Cars*. (Gloucestershire: Sutton Publishing, 2000)

Piggott, Bill, *Triumph: Sport and Elegance*. (Somerset: Haynes Publishing, 2006)

Road & Track on Triumph Sports Cars 1953–1967. (Surrey: Brooklands Books)

Road & Track on Triumph Sports Cars 1967–1974. (Surrey: Brooklands Books)

Road & Track on Triumph Sports Cars 1974–1982. (Surrey: Brooklands Books)

Robson, Graham, *The Story of Triumph Sports Cars*. (Surrey: Motor Racing Publications, 1974)

Robson, Graham, *The Works Triumphs: 50 Years in Motorsport*. (Somerset: Foulis, 1993)

Robson, Graham and Richard Langworth, *Triumph Cars: The Complete Story*. (Croydon, MRP Publishing, 2004)

Robson, Graham, *Works Triumphs in Detail*. (Devon: Herridge & Sons, 2014)

Stein, Jonathan A., *British Sports Cars in America 1946–1981*. (Kutztown: Automobile Quarterly Publications 1993)

Taylor, James, *Triumph Spitfire and GT6: The Complete Story*. (Ramsbury: Crowood Press, 2000)

Thomasen, John, *Triumph Spitfire and GT6: A Guide to Originality*. (Wiltshire: Crowood, 1995)

About the Author

John Nikas is the author of several books, including the award-winning *Rule Britannia: When British Sports Cars Saved a Nation*. A regular contributor to *Triumph World* in the United Kingdom and *The Vintage Triumph Register* in the United States, he has campaigned a number of Triumph models in vintage racing events on both sides of the Atlantic. He is a member of the Guild of Automotive Writers, Society of Automotive Historians, the British Automobile Racing Club and the Friends of Triumph.

About the Photographer

Marc Vorgers (1967) studied industrial design and graduated on innovative transportation solutions in Arnhem, the Netherlands, before starting his own design studio in 1992. In 2000, he founded the Classicar Garage (www.ClassicarGarage.nl), which is one of the automotive world's most visited websites. Marc has profiled thousands of vintage and classic cars, and also contributed photographs, historical information and editorials to publications across the continent and the rest of the world.